READER'S DIGEST

WINNER'S CIRCLE

4

READER'S DIGEST

WINNER'S CIRCLE

Sports stories of inspiration and courage
from America's most popular magazine

THE READER'S DIGEST ASSOCIATION, INC.
Pleasantville, New York/Montreal

Illustrations by Larry Winborg

Library of Congress Cataloging in Publication Data
Reader's digest winner's circle.
       p.   cm.
  ISBN 0-89577-887-4 (pbk.)
  I. Athletes–Biography.   I. Reader's digest.
  GV697. A I R424 1996
  796.092'2–dc20
  [B]   96-14823

Printed in the United States of America

TABLE OF CONTENTS

INTRODUCTION

The blessing of sport is threefold. First, there is the joy that comes to the competitors. Second, there is the joy that accrues to the spectators. And, third, there are the subtle but lasting joys that both participants and observers take from the arena, the nuggets of wisdom that can be pocketed and used for a lifetime as currency in the real world.

This book deals only fleetingly with the first two benefits, since they are best understood at the moment of action, live, as the contest unfolds. It is the third aspect that lends itself best to explanation and celebration through the printed word. A picture may be worth a thousand words, but a sporting event is worth a thousand stories, ten thousand lessons. This book deals with those stories and lessons.

The true tales that follow remind us of why we are mesmerized by sport, why we lose ourselves in playing, watching and thinking about games. These essays remind us that it is sport that gives us the well-lit stage upon which we often act out the themes of our lives, for better or for worse.

Heroes do exist in sport. Unequivocal and grand. They are the ones who use sport for the better, just as great composers use pianos for the better. And it is heroes who are celebrated here.

In the real world losers are everywhere. They crowd around us, murmuring always that this or that thing can't be done, that great effort is futile, that luck is all that counts, and who has much of that anyway? Indeed, we all feel the loser inside ourselves, and we fight against that nasty guy until sometimes we're ready to just fold up and quit. This book is a loser-chaser. Believe me.

You think you've got it bad? For perspective, just read about Brenda Smith, who overcame spina bifida to become a bronze medalist freestyler in the 1992 Paralympic Games. Or check out Jimmie Huega, the Olympic silver medalist skier who was struck down by multiple sclerosis and then rose from his despair to become a symbol of hope and enthusiasm to people with disabilities everywhere.

And I defy anyone to read about Joni Dunn — the athlete who crushed her spine so severely in a skiing accident that she went from being 5'7" tall to 5'3" — and not come away enlightened. Not only did Dunn work for six years rehabilitating herself simply to become normal, but she went on, at age 42, to set a world age-group record in the Ironman Triathlon.

At their root, all of these narratives — even the charming one about a feisty horse named Sunday Silence — are about morality. Simply put: It is good and ethical and right in this world to work hard toward a goal. It is good not to give up. If we do not believe those things, then the world crumbles around us, and life becomes a pointless, sardonic joke.

A sailor crosses the ocean alone, against fearsome winds and waves. An NCAA champion basketball coach battles terminal cancer with such good cheer and enthusiasm that he stuns all the healthy people he meets. A young woman traverses 1,000 miles of frozen land by dogsled, plowing through blizzards and 30-foot snowdrifts. A Major League baseball player named Curtis Pride, who is deaf, is asked how he has withstood the onslaught of his detractors to achieve what he has, and he says, "What matters isn't what *they* think, but what *you* think of *yourself.*"

Clichés? Of course. But what wonderful — and necessary — clichés they are.

I myself had forgotten that much of my own childhood spunk had been cultivated by reading tales about champions over setback. One story in particular that resonated in my young head was that of the ordeal of Jim Cunningham, the runner who had been burned horribly as a child but went on to become a world-class miler. If Jim could do it, I used to tell myself, I could do it, too. What that "it" was, I didn't know. But I felt inspiration flooding through me where once there had been only doubt. "It" would show up sooner or later, I knew.

The story of Mr. Cunningham is not included in this collection (indeed, his tale has been told so many times, it creaks), but there are stories about great modern athletes such as Carl Lewis, Michael Jordan, Kristi Yamaguchi and Mel Blount. There are stories, too, of lesser-known athletes who have overcome everything from blindness to broken bones to crippling diseases, in sports ranging from bicycling to powerboat racing to synchronized swimming. As I read these pieces I felt again the warm inspiration I had once felt as a child. And I realized how sad it is to let such a feeling fade away.

The world does beat us down. But the sweet thing about heroes is that they can lift us back up where we belong. Raise our heads. Get our eyes off the ground and back on the sky, where they should be.

Heroes in all their many venues have risen out of their circumstances and challenges to lead us onward. Sports heroes are no different, except that they rise from the dust of the arena floor to show us the way.

Don't read this book all at once. Take it in chunks and savor them. Think about the lessons implied and how you can use them. Smile a little.

You'll remember that life is good.

Rick Telander

Head Sports Columnist, *Chicago Sun-Times*
Special Contributor, *Sports Illustrated*

HEART OF A CHAMPION

by Pat Busteed

At five feet, ten inches and 108 pounds, Michael was far from a natural. But he was determined to play football.

IN MY THIRD YEAR as head coach of a small high school, I addressed a group of adults and students on the benefits of football. It was the traditional recruitment talk about teamwork and cooperation; I told the crowd that football was not just for star athletes.

Afterward, a couple approached me. Their son, who had had a sickly childhood, really wanted to play football. They had tried to dissuade him. When they told me his name, my heart fell. Michael was five feet, ten inches and weighed about 108 pounds. He was a loner, the brunt of other kids' jokes and snide remarks, and as far as I knew he had never participated in sports.

I stammered through my clichés, trying to tell them it might not be a good idea. But so close on the heels of

Names have been changed to protect privacy.

my "football is for everyone" speech, I said we could give it a try. The opening day of practice, Michael was the first player on the field. We went through 30 minutes of stretching and then a one-mile jog around the track.

Michael began near the back. At 50 yards, he stumbled and fell, and I helped him to his feet. "Michael," I said, "why don't you just walk the laps." He began to get teary-eyed and stammered that he hadn't even tried yet. So I swallowed my heart and sent him on. Repeatedly he fell, each time picking himself up. After one lap, I pulled him aside.

This occurred every day for weeks. During practice I assigned a coach to baby-sit Michael and keep him out of contact drills. It was tough to provide that kind of attention, but Michael's courage and tenacity made it impossible to do anything else.

"Michael," I said, "why don't you just walk the laps." He began to get teary-eyed and stammered that he hadn't even tried yet.

As the season progressed Michael improved, socially and physically. He began to laugh and joke with team members, and most began to see him as some crazy kid brother. Instead of ridiculing him, the kids became touchingly protective.

By the last week of practice Michael ran the mile without falling. We had won only one game that season, yet the team cheered louder for Michael's run than they had during our lone victory.

As I left my office for the last time that season, I was surprised to see Michael standing there. I told him how proud I was of him.

"Coach," he said, "I never played."

I started to say that I didn't want him injured.

Michael stopped me again. "I know why you couldn't play me, but I want you to next year. What can I do?" I told him to stop by my house and I would put together a schedule of weight training and exercises for him.

Michael wasn't in any of my classes, and I really didn't see much of him over the next couple of months, but I'd wave at him every night as I left school. He would be doing sit-ups or running, and it was obvious he was

sticking to the program. Then one night I heard a knock at my door, and there was Michael. He had put on about ten pounds and there seemed to be more color to his face. He wondered if I might beef up the program since it was becoming too easy. I laughed and added a few more exercises and doubled the running.

At the start of the next season, Michael ran the opening mile faster than anyone. Although he had a tough time in the drills, he did a pretty good job.

The following Monday after practice, I ran into one of the team captains. Steve was talented but lazy and undisciplined. He was an honor student who rarely studied and was popular with his peers even though he could be heartless.

Steve pointed to the field where Michael was doing push-ups and asked me why he was still out there. I told Steve to ask him. The next night, I was surprised to see Steve working alongside Michael.

Several weeks later, we were preparing for one of our biggest games, and practice was grueling. I dismissed the team and started in. Only two kids left the field. The rest were huddled around Michael, who was giving them another workout. Steve had called on the players to join Michael and him in their post-practice workouts.

When the game began, we quickly fell behind by two touchdowns, and it was clear some kids had already given up. But not Michael, now an occasional starting guard. He was working so hard and imploring the team so much to keep trying that few had the courage to quit. We won by one point with ten seconds remaining. I picked Michael as player of the week, not so much for his play but because he was obviously the reason the others had kept fighting. We finished the season as one of the top teams in the state.

At the end-of-year banquet, the big award goes to the most productive player based on a strict point system. Although I would have liked to give it to Michael, I knew it belonged to Steve. I called him up to receive it.

"As much as I honor this award," Steve said, "there is someone who deserves it more than I do." The entire crowd went silent. "Everything I accomplished this season, and everything the team accomplished, is due to one person."

He turned to Michael. It was hard for Steve to talk. "Michael, you used to say that I was your hero. If I were half the man you are, I would be proud, because there is no doubt that you are *my* hero."

Michael ran up to the podium and hugged Steve so hard he almost fell down. The entire team cheered.

Michael is in the military today, and I haven't heard from him in years. He and his parents always tried to tell me how much I had helped him. I don't think they realize I was more of a bystander. I know I never found the words to tell Michael that he had done more for me than I had for him.

There are a lot more Michaels out there — kids who will never be "stars" but will probably give and get more from sports than the athletically gifted. It's those kids that sports are for, and those who make me proud to be a coach.

FOREVER "THE BABE"

by Robert W. Creamer

Even today, these many years later, Babe Ruth remains the standard by which excellence is measured.

N 1961 ROGER MARIS broke Babe Ruth's record of 60 home runs in one season. In 1974 Henry Aaron eclipsed Ruth's mark for most home runs in a career — 714. Aaron finally finished well ahead of Ruth, with 755 homers. Yet you don't hear much about Aaron or Maris today. On the other hand, Babe Ruth remains a standard of superiority.

It has been 48 years since Babe Ruth died, 60 years since his last big-league game. Baseball heroes have since come and gone. Yet Babe Ruth's name continues to pop up everywhere, in conversation, speeches, books and movies. In 1995 the Hofstra University Cultural Center on Long Island, N.Y., held an academic conference to commemorate the 100th anniversary of his birth. Why does he have such a hold on the American imagination?

George Herman Ruth was born on February 6, 1895, in Baltimore. His father was a saloonkeeper, and the family lived upstairs over the bar. When he was a small child, Ruth was a holy terror. He played hooky from school, stole fruits and vegetables from stores and drank whiskey he found in his father's bar.

His parents finally committed him to St. Mary's Industrial School for Boys in Baltimore, a training and reform school.

There, taking up baseball, Ruth became a left-handed pitcher and the school's best player. Soon his reputation spread. In February 1914 the Baltimore Orioles — then a minor-league team — signed him to a contract, at $600 for the season.

Ruth's impact was immediate. Barely a week later, he left St. Mary's a professional ballplayer. "The hit will live in the memory of all who saw it," one newspaper account reported. "The ball carried so far to right field that [Ruth] walked around the bases."

Ruth also picked up his indelible nickname. Most of his teammates were much older, and they began calling him Jack Dunn's babe — after the Orioles' owner and manager. Before long, he was Babe Ruth to everybody.

Triumphant Gesture. Ruth always played to the fans. Shortly before the 1914 season, the Orioles went up against the renowned New York Giants in an exhibition game in Baltimore. The last out of Baltimore's 2–1 victory came on a ball thrown to Ruth at first base. Overjoyed by the win, Ruth whooped with pleasure and threw the ball high across the field into the left-field seats. Because baseballs were expensive, things like that just weren't done in those days. Ruth's triumphant gesture was, therefore, an extravagant one — and the Baltimore fans loved it.

Ruth had a tremendous rookie season in 1914. Considered strictly a pitcher, he won 14 games in less than three months before Dunn sold him to the Boston Red Sox in July. Quickly he became the best left-handed pitcher in the American League. He won 18 games in 1915 and 23 in 1916. In the 1918 World Series, he pitched a shutout and won a second game in which he extended his streak of scoreless World Series innings to 29, a record that lasted more than 40 years.

Ruth was also a great batter, however, and by 1919, now primarily a hitter, he broke the major-league record for home runs in one season, smashing 29. The old American League record had been only 16.

Cheerful Booing. Ruth was soon a national celebrity, and the Red Sox owner, desperate for cash, sold him to the New York Yankees. Taking off like a rocket, Ruth hit 54 homers in 1920 and 59 in 1921.

He was colossal, and he played with panache. In the 1921 World Series, the New York Giants seldom threw Ruth a pitch in the strike zone. In one game, after receiving his third consecutive base on balls, he suddenly bolted for second. That stunned the Giants and the crowd. Moments later he stole third base too. Even with a beer belly, he was a beautifully coordinated athlete, and he went on to steal 123 bases in his career.

Before long, Ruth was even delighting the fans of opposing teams. In the 1928 World Series in St. Louis, he was booed cheerfully by Cardinal fans when he took his place in left field during the final game. (You can boo cheerfully.) Ruth grinned at the crowd and pointed to right field in a gesture that clearly said, "I'm going to hit one out there." He did hit one out, then another and another—the second time he'd hit three homers in one World Series game.

With the Yankees leading in the last half of the ninth inning with two out, the final St. Louis batter hit a foul fly down the left-field line, where extra seats had been placed for the overflow crowd. From left field, Ruth ran in along the temporary fence in front of the seats—while St. Louis fans whacked at him with programs to keep him from making the catch. Reaching above their heads, he deftly plucked the ball out of the air. It was the last out of the Series, and as he ran toward the dugout, Ruth held the ball high in the air, waving it like a trophy. It was in enemy territory with an enemy crowd, but the fans loved it.

Fights and Suspensions. At this stage in his career, however, Ruth repeatedly got into trouble — for bad-mouthing umpires, for trying to punch one, for climbing into the grandstand to go after an abusive fan. In 1922 he was suspended five times. In 1925 he drank too much, slept too little, quarreled with his manager, was suspended again and was slapped with a $5,000 fine — an enormous sum at that time. Now past 30, he looked terrible and was overweight. Many people thought he was a rocket that had burned out.

Amazingly, though, The Babe was still fun to be around, which may explain something about his broad appeal. Once, probing for an adverse opinion, I asked an old-time player, "Why did some people dislike Ruth?"

"Dislike him?" he said. "People got mad at him, but I never heard of anybody who didn't like Babe Ruth."

He finally straightened himself out, and from 1926 through 1931, as he aged from 31 to 36, he put on the best sustained streak of power hitting that baseball has ever seen. In 1927 he hit his famous 60 home runs, but almost as impressive is the fact that during those six seasons he *averaged* 50 homers a year. He led the American League in home runs 12 times in 14 seasons.

For all his carefree ways, Ruth almost always retained a sense of obligation to his role as a hero, off the field as well as on.

Last Hurrah. Ruth began slowing down in 1932, although he still hit 41 home runs. In September he suffered what appeared to be an attack of appendicitis, and it was thought he might not make the World Series that fall against the Chicago Cubs. But Ruth played every game of the Series, batting .333.

In the third game he hit two homers, one of them his most famous home run ever — the legendary Called Shot. That was when he defied the hooting Chicago crowd, made a sweeping motion toward center field and smashed one of the longest home runs ever hit in Wrigley Field. I don't believe he pointed to the spot he planned to hit the ball, as legend has it, but there is no doubt in my mind he indicated he was going to hit one.

Ruth followed that up with a couple of declining years with the Yankees and then, in 1935, with the old Boston Braves. His muscles ached, his eyes hurt and his batting average fell well below .200. He wanted to retire, but the Braves' owner asked him to make one last attendance-boosting road trip with the club. Ruth agreed.

Toward the end of the trip, in a game in Pittsburgh, he roused himself and hit three home runs, the final one a monumental drive over the roof in right field. "I'm telling you, it was the longest cockeyed ball I ever saw in my life," said the opposing pitcher, Guy Bush.

This was Ruth's last home run and last base hit. When the Braves returned home to Boston, he left the team for good.

Sense of Duty. For all his carefree ways, Ruth almost always retained a sense of obligation to his role as a hero, off the field as well as on. In 1947, ill with cancer but still traveling, he was staying in a Cincinnati hotel suite when Waite Hoyt, a former New York Yankees teammate, came to visit him. Hoyt brought along his wife, whom he had married not long before. When the Hoyts started to leave, Ruth said, "Wait a minute," and got painfully to his feet, limped into the kitchen and came out holding a small vase with an orchid in it. "Here," he said to Mrs. Hoyt, referring to her recent wedding, "I never gave you anything."

He had that same sense of duty when he was close to death in the summer of 1948. He left his hospital room to attend the première of the Babe Ruth movie starring William Bendix. Once the film began, Ruth grew uncomfortable, and he left before it was over. Back in the hospital he said, "All my obligations are over. I'm going to rest now." He died three weeks later.

Babe Ruth was the best baseball player who ever lived. He was head and shoulders over everyone else. He was also the most flamboyant, the most fun to watch. And that, I suppose, is why the amazing Babe still maintains a powerful grip on America's imagination.

THE IRON COURAGE OF JONI DUNN

by John G. Hubbell

A patch of ice on a ski slope sent the gritty athlete plunging out of control and into the greatest challenge of her life.

SUDDENLY Joni Dunn was in midair, plunging off the side of Stratton Mountain, Vt., into a jagged ravine filled with a wilderness of trees and scrub bush. Frightened as she had never been before, Joni watched the world rushing up to meet her. The young skier tried to twist to avoid a large tree, wrenching her body so violently that she actually heard bones breaking in her back. The tree slammed against her right side, then her back, and finally smashed against her head.

Then it was over—and Joni had never felt better. She was in an immense and glorious place, suffused with a lovely symphony of colors. There was perfect peace here, a transcendent happiness. In an instant Joni saw everyone and everything that had been important in her life. She felt no pain, remembered no problems. She was drawn toward a brilliant white light and she wanted to reach it more than anything she had ever wanted before. Joni began moving toward it.

This is wonderful! she thought. *So peaceful, so free, so good.* Then another image intruded: her three-year-old son, Bryan, waiting for her at home. *There's nobody to look after Bryan. I can't be dead! I've got to go back to him.*

Joni turned from the mesmerizing light, opened her eyes to the blood-stained snow and knew that she was badly hurt. She wondered if she was paralyzed, but found she could wiggle a foot. Then she felt a fierce, hot pain growing inside her chest. On the trail high above, near the patch of ice that had sent her flying out of control, her skiing companion, Michael Schreder, was screaming, "Ski Patrol! Ski Patrol!"

Soon four ski patrolmen had inched down the ravine, lifted Joni onto a backboard and carried her off the mountain. X rays at the hospital revealed a fractured skull and spine, neck fractures, three broken ribs, a collapsed lung and six shattered vertebrae. Bone fragments had cut into blood vessels and were impinging on her spinal column. Her vital signs were deteriorating, and the doctor felt she could not live out the night.

To relieve her agonizing pain, morphine was prescribed. It relaxed Joni, but she fought sleep, believing that if she drifted off she would not wake. And for Bryan's sake she could not allow herself to die.

All that first night of January 29, 1972, Joni kept telling herself, *I'm going to make it to morning.* At last, first light reached the window, and Joni exulted, telling a nurse, "Now I know I'm going to make it!"

> *Beyond putting her in traction, Joni's doctors could do nothing until she stabilized. It was up to Joni to work a miracle of will.*

Beyond putting her in traction, Joni's doctors could do nothing until she stabilized. It was up to Joni to work a miracle of will. She lay in her web of traction, hurting, napping involuntarily, waking herself, thinking about Bryan. She spent the night hours looking for dawn, praying for it, thanking God each time it came.

The Hardest Step. A week passed, and Joni seemed stronger. Although the broken ribs and the hot pain in her chest made breathing difficult, the certainty grew in her that she would survive. Still she worried about the kind of life that lay before her.

Joni, 29, had come east from Indiana in 1966, and was a medical technologist at Greenwich Hospital in Connecticut. But how was she to work now? Pay the bills? Take care of Bryan? Her former husband, Bryan's father, was struggling with a new career and wouldn't be able to help.

Susan and Renny Warren, friends who were looking after Bryan, brought him to visit. "You can't touch her," Susan explained to Bryan, holding him up so Joni could see him. "I'm okay, Bryan," Joni told him. "Everything is going to be all right."

After three weeks Joni was transferred to Greenwich Hospital. Bryan was brought for frequent visits and spoke to his mother by telephone daily. Joni's friend Michael Schreder assured her that when she left the hospital, his parents wanted to look after her.

Six weeks after the accident, Joni was taken out of traction and put in a body brace extending from her neck to the tops of her thighs. Each day her bed was cranked up gradually, until she was able to sit up straight. One day she was allowed to put her legs over the side of the bed; the next she was asked to stand and take a step. She looked down at her tingling feet, concentrated hard and with a tremendous effort slid her right foot forward.

Joni added shuffling steps each day. The pain contin-ued to burn in her chest, but except for two crushed vertebrae, which doctors had not been able to salvage, the fractures all had healed. She learned to get in and out of her body brace without help. On warm spring days she was able to take short walks outdoors. Soon she was discharged.

High-Risk Surgery. In her body brace Joni was able to stand up straight, but when she removed it, her body sagged forward; her upper back hunched grotesquely.

She had been five feet, seven inches tall before the accident. Now she stood barely five feet, three inches.

The Warrens insisted on keeping Bryan until Joni was capable of looking after him. Meanwhile, Joni spent a lot of time in the Schreders' pool, paddling, trying to build up her strength. She also took walks every day.

In July, Joni met with Dr. Hugo Keim, a noted orthopedic surgeon and chief of the Spine Service at New York City's Columbia Presbyterian Medical Center. Keim thought he might be able to straighten her back, though it would involve high-risk surgery. Joni could come out of it a paraplegic or could die on the table. If the operation worked, she would have to spend a year in a body cast. "There are no guarantees," Keim emphasized. "Go home and think about it."

"I don't have to think about it," Joni replied. "I want the surgery."

Keim operated in September. He used slivers shaved from the pelvis to fuse the vertebrae together, thus straightening and supporting the spine. Joni was on the table nine hours and needed 12 pints of blood.

When she awakened, the nurses were smiling, and she noticed that her chest pain was gone. Dr. Keim assured her that the operation had gone well. In a few days, when the surgical wounds had healed, he would put her in a body cast and send her home.

Joni convalesced for two months, worrying about being dependent on others. The accident had cost her apartment, her furniture, her car — eventually she feared she might be judged incapable of raising Bryan. But she was determined to regain her independence.

Her right foot still shuffled slightly, but she was able to walk, and felt strong enough for part-time work. Greenwich Hospital took her on again as a medical technologist.

As the months passed, Joni gained strength and confidence. She rented a small apartment for herself and Bryan. A year after the operation, Dr. Keim removed the body cast. Joni stood gazing at herself in a full-length mirror, amazed, overjoyed. At five feet, five inches — Keim had given her back two inches in height — she looked normal; her shoulders remained rounded, and the hunch was nearly gone.

A year after the operation, Dr. Keim removed the body cast. Joni stood gazing at herself in a full-length mirror, amazed, overjoyed.

Running to Daylight. A year in the body cast had weakened Joni's back muscles, and she was in pain. On the advice of her doctors, she went to the YWCA every day and learned how to swim free-style. Her back pain disappeared, and she began to notice muscle tone in her arms and upper body that hadn't been there before.

In 1976, Joni took a job at Greenwich Country Day School, where she taught science and coached field hockey. While refereeing a scrimmage, she discovered that it no longer hurt to run. Soon she was doing laps with the girls.

Joni wanted to try running seriously. That winter at the Y, she overcame the embarrassment of her round shoulders and unrhythmic gait, and set out on the track.

She struggled for breath, hurting, but kept going. She forced herself to come back for more, week after week. When the weather got warmer, she began running outdoors. Eventually she was running five miles at a stretch, loving how strong and alive it made her feel. And she noticed that her shoulders were straightening.

In 1978 Joni entered the Greenwich five-mile Memorial Day race. She was nervous. After all, she was 35, had spent six years recovering from a frightful accident, had never before competed in an athletic event. But Bryan would be waiting for her at the finish line. She went ahead with it, and finished first in the 30-to-39 age division. At the awards ceremony, nine-year-old Bryan was misty-eyed with pride. The ability to give him such a moment was the best medicine Joni had ever had. She resolved to race again.

Joni began running longer stretches. In 1979 she ran in the New York City Marathon and again competed in the race the following year. And in 1982 she qualified for the Boston Marathon.

Among the runners on the roads around Greenwich was Mark MacIntyre. In 1983 he finished sixth in the Iron Man Triathlon World Championship in Hawaii, a grueling event that comprises a 2.4-mile ocean swim, a 112-mile bicycle race, and a marathon. Joni admired what MacIntyre had accomplished. She bought a magazine about triathlons, began swimming again at the Y and purchased a racing bike.

Joni entered a triathlon in April 1985 in Tampa, Fla., where there would be no friends to see her fail. It involved a one-mile swim, a 25-mile bicycle race and a 10-kilometer (6.2-mile) run.

Wading toward the starting line in Tampa Bay, she thought, *This is stupid. You don't belong here. You're 42 years old.*

At the signal, Joni dived ahead, trying to swim, but all around her people were hitting, kicking, fighting to get out front. Panicking, she stopped swimming and stood up, turning toward the shore. *But you've been through so much,* she told herself. *And think what this means to Bryan. Don't give up!*

Joni turned seaward again. She found her rhythm and felt strong as she reached the marker a half-mile out and turned for shore. When she came out of the water, she was amazed to see that many swimmers were behind her.

After pedaling hard on her bicycle for 25 miles, Joni began the 10-kilometer run. Wobbly from biking, she began slowly. But after a mile and a half, she felt as if she could run all day.

At the finish line Joni was euphoric — she had done it! Then, over the loudspeaker came an announcement: "Winner, women's forty-to-forty-four age group, Joni Dunn of Greenwich, Connecticut."

Joni now wanted to test herself to the limit: compete in the 1985 championship triathlon in Hawaii.

Iron Woman. Joni now wanted to test herself to the limit: compete in the 1985 championship triathlon in Hawaii. She enlisted Mark MacIntyre as her coach. Mark put Joni on a high-carbohydrate diet and a rigorous daily training schedule.

Joni and Mark reached Hawaii 18 days before the race to get Joni acclimated to the windy, mountainous routes. On the morning of October 26, a cannon shot sent 1,018 people into the water off the Kona Coast. Joni swam strongly. She had planned that the swim would take two hours, but when she came out of the water, she was 32 minutes ahead of schedule!

She took off on her bike. Mark would be waiting at the top of the first hill, and she was anxious to see his reaction to her time. He was overjoyed. "I'm having a great time!" Joni shouted as she sped by.

Mark and Joni had figured that the 112-mile bicycle ride would take her 7 to 7½ hours. She completed it in 6 hours and 19 minutes — but stressed a tendon behind her right ankle. "Run as far as you can, then walk," Mark told her as she began the last event.

Joni eased into the marathon, refusing to let herself think about her sore ankle. There were aid stations every mile. She did not stop running until she reached the 14th. There, she drank some water and realized that her ankle didn't hurt anymore. She ran to the next aid station, walked a short distance, then ran two miles and walked again.

She knew when she was atop the final hill — she could "smell" the finish line ahead. Mark watched her come on, astounded at her finishing kick. As she crossed the line, her number was called: "325, Joni Dunn, Greenwich, Connecticut." Then — "Women's forty-to-forty-four age group, first finisher."

Her time: 12 hours, 3 minutes, 26 seconds. Not only had she won the championship; she had beaten the world record for her age group by some 20 minutes!

Joni Dunn has come a long way since deciding not to die in that ravine on Stratton Mountain. She continues to race in triathlons, but also likes to talk to young people about how to get the most out of themselves and out of life, about patience, planning and determination. "Don't take a single day for granted," she tells them. "Make the best of every moment."

One thing she doesn't have to talk about is courage — the kind that makes miracles happen.

SPIRIT OF THE OLYMPICS

"The essential thing is not to have conquered but to have fought well," the Olympic creed states. These seven athletes have more than lived up to the Games' high goal.

"I'LL GET ANOTHER ONE"

SEOUL — At his father's funeral, American Carl Lewis placed his 100-meter gold medal from the 1984 Olympics in his father's hands. "Don't worry," he told his surprised mother. "I'll get another one."

A year later, in the 100-meter final at the 1988 games, Lewis was competing against Canadian world-record-holder Ben Johnson. Halfway through the race Johnson was five feet in front. Lewis was convinced he could catch him. But at 80 meters, he was still five feet behind. *It's over, Dad,* Lewis thought. As Johnson crossed the finish, he stared back at Lewis and thrust his right arm in the air, index finger extended.

Lewis was exasperated. He had noticed Johnson's bulging muscles and yellow-tinged eyes, both indications of steroid use. "I didn't have the medal, but I could still give to my father by acting with class and dignity," Lewis said later. He shook Johnson's hand and left the track.

But then came the announcement that Johnson had tested positive for anabolic steroids. He was stripped of his medal. The gold went to Lewis, a replacement for the medal he had given his father.

— David Wallechinsky in *The Complete Book of the Olympics*

REMARKABLE LEAP

BERLIN — Jesse Owens seemed sure to win the long jump at the 1936 games. The year before he had jumped 26 feet, 8¼ inches — a record that would stand

for 25 years. As he walked to the long-jump pit, however, Owens saw a tall, blue-eyed, blond German taking practice jumps in the 26-foot range. Owens felt nervous. He was acutely aware of the Nazis' desire to prove "Aryan superiority," especially over blacks.

On his first jump Owens inadvertently leaped from several inches beyond the takeoff board. Rattled, he fouled on his second attempt too. He was one foul away from being eliminated.

At this point, the tall German introduced himself as Luz Long. "You should be able to qualify with your eyes closed!" he said to Owens, referring to his two jumps.

For the next few moments the black son of a share-cropper and the white model of Nazi manhood chatted. Then Long made a suggestion. Since the qualifying distance was only 23 feet, 5½ inches, why not make a mark several inches before the takeoff board and jump from there, just to play it safe? Owens did so, and he qualified easily.

In the finals Owens set an Olympic record and earned the second of four golds. The first person to congratulate him was Luz Long — in full view of Adolf Hitler.

Owens never again saw Long, who was killed in World War II. "You could melt down all the medals and cups I have," Owens later wrote, "and they wouldn't be a plating on the 24-carat friendship I felt for Luz Long."
— David Wallechinsky in *The Complete Book of the Olympics*

> *For the next few moments the black son of a sharecropper and the white model of Nazi manhood chatted.*

GALLANT ACT

SEOUL — Sailing competitions were under way at Pusan on September 24, 1988, with winds raging at 35 knots and playing havoc with the boats. Two sailors of the Singapore team, Joseph Chan and Shaw Her, were thrown overboard when their boat capsized.

Canada's Lawrence Lemieux was sailing alone nearby in a separate event when he saw the sailors in distress.

He rescued Chan, who was exhausted from struggling against the strong currents in his weighted sailing jacket. By the time Lemieux finished helping the Singapore team, he had fallen well behind in his race.

Judges awarded Lemieux second place — the position he was in when he went to the sailors' aid — and the International Olympic Committee gave him a special award for his gallantry.

"It's the first rule of sailing to help people in distress," said Lemieux, downplaying the incident.

—Bud Greenspan in *Parade*

> *... they noticed that the child's feet turned inward, the toes facing each other. Carole was determined to do whatever it would take to help her daughter walk normally.*

PROUDEST MOMENT

ALBERTVILLE — In 1942, hysteria over Japanese involvement in World War II led to the relocation of some 110,000 Japanese Americans to internment camps. In one of these camps Carole Doi, a third-generation Japanese American, was born. Despite this experience, Carole was proud to have been born in America.

Years later, Carole married a man who had also spent time in the camps. When she delivered their baby daughter, they noticed that the child's feet turned inward, the toes facing each other. Carole was determined to do whatever it would take to help her daughter walk normally.

For four years Carole had to provide the child with corrective shoes. Her daughter was walking normally by age six, but Carole wasn't satisfied. "I wanted her to do anything in which she would use her legs," she says. The girl chose ice skating.

Before long, the youngster was bugging her mother for more rink time. She'd refuse to leave the ice until she got a particular move right. Soon Carole was rising at 4 A.M. to get her daughter to the rink. Finally, after 15 years of lessons, young Kristi Yamaguchi represented her country in the Olympics.

As the U.S. flag was hoisted during the 1992 medals ceremony, Carole and Jim Yamaguchi watched Kristi receive the gold medal. They had never been so proud to be Americans.
— Keith A. White

UNEXPECTED HELP

INNSBRUCK — In 1964, Italy's Eugenio Monti and Sergio Siorpaes were heavily favored in the two-man bobsled event. But as they awaited their second run, the lightly regarded British team of Tony Nash and Robin Dixon was in a state of despair. After a sensational first run, their sled had broken an axle bolt, and it seemed certain they would have to drop out.

Monti, his second run already completed, acted swiftly. He stripped the bolt from his own sled and offered it to Nash. In one of the greatest upsets in the history of the Olympics, the British team went on to win the gold medal, while the sportsmanlike Monti finished third.

Four years later, Monti drove both his two- and four-man sleds to Olympic victory.
— Bud Greenspan in *Parade*

GOING THE DISTANCE

TOKYO — American discus-thrower Al Oerter is the only athlete in history to win the same track-and-field event in four successive Olympiads. The one he prizes most came at Tokyo in 1964, when he was going for his third victory.

A week before the games, Oerter tore the cartilage in his rib cage. The team doctor ordered him to rest, which meant Oerter was out of the competition. However, Oerter arrived at the finals with tape and ice bags, determined to compete.

Each finals competitor is allowed six throws, the longest of which wins. After four rounds, Oerter was in so much pain he decided his fifth throw would be his last. As he turned and let the discus fly, he doubled over in agony. When the distance was announced, Oerter

learned that he had set a new Olympic record — one that none of his competitors could best.

"Given any other environment, I would have stopped," Oerter said afterward. "But these were the Olympic games, and you die for them."
— Bud Greenspan in *Parade*

TRIUMPH, AT LAST

SEOUL — In 1910, Japan annexed Korea as a colony and set about obliterating the Korean culture. Running became one of the only ways Koreans could compete with the despised Japanese and continue to identify themselves as Koreans.

Sohn Kee Chung
Korean medalist

One young runner, Sohn Kee Chung, trained hard along the banks of the Yalu River, with sand in his pants and rocks on his back. But he knew the only way he could win would be to run under the flag of imperialistic Japan. In 1936, Sohn bested the Japanese competition at the Olympic tryouts for the marathon; reluctantly, the Japanese sent him to Berlin.

Sohn was given a Japanese name, Kitei Son. But when he signed in, he wrote his Korean name.

Sohn won the race in Olympic record time. At the medal ceremony, during the raising of the Japanese flag, Sohn bowed his head in protest.

Sohn's true celebration came at the beginning of the 1988 games, when the 76-year-old entered the Seoul stadium bearing the Olympic torch. In a moment that brought tears to the entire crowd, Sohn bounded around the track, leaping for joy and bursting with pride for himself and his country.

> *Sohn's true celebration came . . .*
>
> *when the 76-year-old entered*
>
> *the Seoul stadium bearing*
>
> *the Olympic torch.*

— Ron Fimrite in *Sports Illustrated* and David Wallechinsky in *The Complete Book of the Olympics*

UNFORGETTABLE ARTHUR ASHE

by Charles Pasarell

**Stay with it, the great tennis player's
life says to us — you can go all the way.**

'LL NEVER FORGET the time Arthur Ashe played Ilie Nastase in the 1975 Masters tennis tournament in Stockholm, Sweden. Nastase was always volatile, but this day he was out of control — stalling, cursing and taunting Ashe like a madman. Finally Ashe put down his racket and walked off the court.

"I've had enough," he told the umpire. "I'm at the point where I'm afraid I'll lose control."

The umpire was shocked; Ashe was winning. "But Arthur," he pleaded, "you'll default the match."

"I don't care," Ashe said. "I'd rather lose that than my self-respect."

The following day, the tournament committee met. By disqualifying Ashe, they'd be condoning Nastase's bullying tactics. And wasn't how you played the game what really counted? Arthur had that way of making you confront yourself.

The officials decided it was Nastase who must default the match for his unsportsmanlike conduct.

Arthur Ashe was the most courageous man I ever knew, always holding himself and others to the highest standards.

We first met when we played against each other in Miami's Orange Bowl Junior Tennis Tournament. It often surprised me that two 12-year-olds from such different backgrounds could become lifelong friends. I was born into a well-to-do family and played my first tennis at country clubs with my father. Arthur grew up less privileged and played at segregated facilities. His mother died when he was six, and his dad knew nothing of tennis.

Arthur grew up less privileged and played at segregated facilities. His mother died when he was six, and his dad knew nothing of tennis.

But ours was a friendship based on more than tennis. If I marveled as he scaled the heights of professional sports, what impressed me more was how he used dignity and restraint as weapons against opponents, whether childish tennis players or the cruel purveyors of racism. With his poker-faced courage he stared down social injustice, three heart attacks and AIDS, and became a conscience for a nation.

"No Hanging Around." When Arthur was four, his father, a parks policeman in Richmond, Va., was put in charge of Brook Field, the city's largest playground for blacks. The Ashes moved into a five-room home in the middle of the 18-acre park. Suddenly Arthur's "back yard" included a swimming pool, basketball courts, baseball fields — and tennis courts.

When he began playing, he was so small the racket dwarfed him. But by age 13, he was consistently beating players twice his size and age.

The root of Arthur's success was his focus and incredible drive. At 5 A.M. each summer day, he'd hit 500 balls, eat breakfast and hit 500 more.

This capacity for hard work was a legacy of his father, Arthur Sr. In addition to his full-time responsibilities at Brook Field, he ran landscape and janitorial businesses, contracted with a realty firm, did catering and chauffering. When Interstate 95 was being built through Richmond, Arthur Sr. scrounged scrap lumber and bricks from torn-down buildings and, with Arthur and his younger brother Johnnie, built a new home in the country.

These humble beginnings belied Arthur's deep sense of heritage. On his father's side, the family traces its line back through an early governor of North Carolina to a slave woman brought from western Africa in 1735 to Yorktown, Va., where she was traded for a bundle of tobacco.

Arthur once recalled, "My father's sense of discipline was simple: He knew what was best for his children, and he had only to give an order once. One of his commandments was, 'There's to be no hanging around. If he ain't workin' or someplace special, a man is supposed to be home.'" He knew the boys' route home from school took exactly 12 minutes — he had paced it off himself — and when Arthur and Johnnie were late, they had to have a good explanation.

"You gain by helping others," their father would say. Matching deed to word, Arthur Sr., with sons in tow, delivered old clothes, food and wood to families in need. And: "You don't get nowhere by making enemies." Those homilies and examples, repeated throughout Arthur's early years, served him well.

"Above all," Arthur remembered, "my father drummed into me that without your good name, you would be nothing. It meant you were letting everybody down — your friends, your family, your history."

I will never forget how Arthur once spoke about something questionable someone had done. "I couldn't possibly do that," he said. "I couldn't face my father if I did."

Asked once if he remembered his mother, Mattie, who died when he was six from complications related to a toxemic pregnancy, Arthur said: "Oh, sure. I remember she taught me to read when I was four.

And she taught me manners, and she taught me about angels."

Gibraltar and Neverland. Arthur was ten when he was introduced to Robert Walter Johnson, a Lynchburg, Va., physician who ran a tennis camp for black youngsters denied access to "white" courts. Besides honing his basic skills, Johnson helped develop Arthur's "inner" game. Never lose your cool, he taught. Raging at the linesman or an opponent was a waste of energy that should be put into the game. Other players' fathers would say to Johnson, "My son was going to pieces. Your player never changed expression."

It did not take Johnson long to see that the skinny youngster had the potential to be great. By 1960, Arthur had won his first title, the National Junior Indoor Championship, and he was offered a tennis scholarship to U.C.L.A. In 1965, Arthur led the school to the NCAA title. The next year he graduated with a degree in business administration.

> *It did not take Johnson long to see that the skinny youngster had the potential to be great.*

On the pro circuit, Arthur was an instant sensation. In the final of the 1968 U.S. Open, he served 26 aces and beat Holland's Tom Okker. It was the first time a black man had won one of tennis's four major tournaments. Then in 1970 he won the Australian Open, the next year — with partner Marty Riessen — the French Open doubles title and in 1975 the Wimbledon singles crown. He was twice ranked No. 1 in the world. Arthur also played on four U.S. Davis Cup championship teams and captained the team to titles in 1981 and 1982.

Arthur's style and quality permeated his life off the court too. So it was no surprise that he was named president of the Association of Tennis Professionals in 1974, for he cared deeply about all players — a rare attitude among prima donna pros.

This extraordinary concern for others was shared by Arthur's wife, Jeanne Moutoussamy, whom he married in 1977. Before their marriage, although Arthur was almost always on the road, he maintained the link with

Jeanne by a steady stream of notes and letters, discussing the big issues before them or just the day-to-day events of their lives.

Jeanne was Arthur's Rock of Gibraltar, and their daughter, Camera, born in 1986, his Neverland — the magic in his eyes. There is a photo Jeanne took of Arthur and Camera that speaks volumes of the devotion he felt for her. Arthur is helping Camera with her golf swing. The ball is surrounded by divots, where the club had missed. Yet the two remain focused and cheerful. *Stay with it*, the picture seems to say, *you'll make it.*

Arthur was always encouraging others. Though Stan Smith was a rival, he was also a friend. So after Stan suffered a devastating first-round loss at the Australian Open one year, Arthur slipped a note under his door, telling him not to lose heart or faith in himself. To this day, Stan can't tell that story without getting choked up. I still cherish the telegram I received from Arthur when I first played Wimbledon in 1967. "You can go all the way!" Arthur assured me. I didn't, but that was Arthur, always there for me.

> *Though Stan Smith was a rival, he was also a friend. So after Stan suffered a devastating first-round loss ...Arthur slipped a note under his door, telling him not to lose heart or faith in himself.*

Once, talking with inner-city kids, he asked, "What do you want to be?"

"Michael Jordan," answered one.

"Why not *own* the team that has Michael Jordan?" replied Arthur.

Later, to help broaden children's horizons, he started the Safe Passage Foundation. The organization has instructed over 3,000 poor youngsters in tennis, golf and fencing, as well as in basic scholastic skills.

Black and White. Arthur used his nationally syndicated newspaper column and his TV appearances on ABC and the cable channel Home Box Office to speak out for racial equality. Through it all, however, he spurned black separatism. Arthur wanted to unite, not divide.

"Some blacks — and some whites too — get mad because they feel I don't make enough waves," Arthur wrote in his 1975 book, *Portrait in Motion.* "There are many ways of accomplishing things in the white world without compromising integrity."

One evening in the 1970s Arthur was in a friend's home in Atlanta when he was challenged by Jesse Jackson. "You're not arrogant enough, Arthur," Jackson declared.

Arthur fixed him with a stare. "You're right, Jesse," he responded. "I'm not arrogant. But I don't think that my lack of arrogance lessens my effectiveness one bit."

All his life Arthur fought to bring blacks and whites together. In 1973, he broke the color line on the courts of South Africa, a country he returned to on several occasions — not just to meet with black leaders, but to visit the youngsters of Soweto as well. Later, he was arrested for protesting apartheid and was instrumental in having South Africa banned from the Davis Cup.

At the same time, Arthur disdained the political correctness that tried to explain away every wrongdoing as an act beyond the individual's control or responsibility. "Poverty, the deterioration of schools and the proliferation of single-parent families are factors, of course," Arthur said. "Still, there are not enough people who will stand up and say, 'That's wrong.'"

During the 1992 Los Angeles riots, Arthur was shamed by those who threw rocks and burned buildings under the guise of fighting racism. "That's not us!" he shouted at the television screen. "Society may have done us wrong," he later said, "but there's no excuse for that."

Arthur also exploded when some black leaders and educators opposed an NCAA rule — Proposition 42 — that denies college scholarships to athletes who do not meet minimum test scores and academic standards. To blacks who said the proposal was racially biased, he countered that the more that was expected of black (and white) kids, the more they would demand of themselves. But he also castigated white administrators: "You don't really care about us as students. You care about us as athletes to fill your stadiums and arenas."

Make Death Blink. Even after leaving the pro-tennis tour, Arthur played regularly and stayed remarkably fit. So it was a staggering blow when I heard of his first heart attack in 1979 at age 36. He underwent bypass surgery that year and again in 1983. Recovery after the second operation seemed particularly slow, so Arthur agreed to receive a few extra units of blood as a boost. Five years later, his right hand went limp, and emergency surgery revealed the cause: AIDS.

For 3½ years Arthur kept his illness to himself, his wife and a few friends. He revealed it on April 8, 1992, only when he learned that USA Today intended to print a story about his condition, if the newspaper could find confirmation. I received a phone call that day from Arthur, asking me to attend his afternoon press conference. Many of us thought that in exchange for the public's supposed "right to know," the rights of a man, his wife and child to privacy were being trampled underfoot.

What Arthur accomplished in his last ten months still amazes me. Despite being weak from his illness, he continued helping children, working to give haven to Haitian refugees, fighting racial injustice and battling AIDS. Facing death, Arthur hoped to make it blink.

"It doesn't frighten me," he told me. "If I asked, 'Why me?' about my troubles, I would have to ask, 'Why me?' about my blessings. Why my winning Wimbledon? Why my marrying a beautiful, gifted woman and having a wonderful child?"

Often during those days, Camera would jump into his lap, then kiss him as he took pills, sipped water and shot AIDS medication into his mouth. Two months before his death, he bought a doll house for her and worked hard to finish it.

Arthur wanted to see Camera go to dances, enter college and marry — all the things his mother didn't live to see him do. In 1991, he walked with her hand-in-hand around the grounds of Wimbledon's All-England Club. "I just wanted her to see where Daddy played," he said, because he knew he might not be back.

On February 5, 1993, Arthur checked into the hospital. The next day, he died.

"You come to realize that life is short," he told a friend, "and you have to step up. Don't feel sorry for me. Much is expected of those who are strong."

A life ends, but values endure.

Arthur Sr. used to tell a story about how his son first responded to the news that his mother had died. The father sat on his son's bed, weeping. "Don't cry, Daddy," the boy told him. "As long as we have each other, we'll be all right."

As long as we have each other. Two days before he died, Arthur finished his last book, *Days of Grace*. The final chapter is a letter to Camera. "Don't be angry with me if I am not there in person, alive and well, when you need me," he writes. "I would like nothing more. When you feel sick at heart and weary of life, or when you stumble and fall and don't know if you can get up again, think of me. I will be watching and smiling and cheering you on."

> *"You come to realize that life is short," he told a friend, "and you have to step up. Don't feel sorry for me. Much is expected of those who are strong."*

BORN TO RACE

by Katie McCabe

Brenda Smith dreamed of becoming a champion athlete. But she would first have to overcome formidable personal challenges.

BRENDA SMITH, in lane three," the voice boomed over the loud-speaker. The crowd cheered, and Brenda's heart began pounding in her throat. She eyed the Australian and German freestylers whose records had stunned her when she arrived in Barcelona to compete in the 1992 Paralympic Games — the world's premier competition for disabled athletes.

Now, as she peered down the 50 meters that lay between her and a medal, time stopped. From a distance of 26 years, she heard the shout of a little girl named Brenda Levy, born with spina bifida.

"I'm going to jump, and you can't stop me!" Everyone froze at the Silver Spring, Md., pool on that June morning of 1966. Brenda Levy, a beautiful eight-year-old with black pigtails and naughty brown eyes, teetered on the high dive. Her crutches lay at the bottom of the ladder.

In unison, the child's mother, Gladys Levy, and her aunt and uncle, Roz and Mel Schuldenfrei, shouted, "Brenda! Not the high dive!"

Brenda grinned wickedly. Nothing made her want to do something more than being told she couldn't. What was another spanking compared with being able to fly 20 feet in the air? Whooping with delight, she sailed out over the water.

When she surfaced, unhurt, her Uncle Mel was shaking his head. He didn't realize what he'd unlocked that morning with his casual "How would you like to learn to swim?"

For Brenda, being born with spina bifida — or "open spine" — meant hauling around 20 pounds of metal leg braces and crutches. Though it did not cause total paralysis, the imperfect closure of the discs at the base of her spine had left her with limited muscular control below the waist and an awkward, waddling gait.

But in the water, her awkwardness turned to grace. For the first time in her life, it was not the weakness in her legs that counted, but the strength in her arms and shoulders.

Brenda had seen the Olympic Games on TV and thrilled to the images of swimmers competing for medals. As she practiced that summer, visions of those swimmers danced in her imagination. *Someday, I'll be one of them,* she thought. As long as she didn't tell anyone what she fantasized, Brenda figured, they couldn't tell her that people with physical disabilities did not become athletes, let alone Olympians.

When she was ten, Brenda tried out for the community pool's swim team. "Those of you who make the A team will be our starters. If you need more work, you'll swim on B team," the coach explained. As Brenda stood in line, her head filled with all the things she wanted to tell the coach. *So what if I can't balance well enough to start off the diving blocks? I'll make it up in the water. Just give me a chance on A team, and I'll work my heart out!*

But the coach saw a kid who walked like a duck. The fact that she could also swim like one didn't seem to count. "Brenda: B team!"

Second best, she thought angrily.

Her parents had always told her, "You can do anything you want to do." So she worked on her timing, her freestyle form and her breathing until she could hold her own with the top swimmers. But the coach never noticed.

Then, when she turned 14, the swimming came to a terrifying halt. For weeks that summer, Brenda had been nauseated, achy, feverish. When her fever spiked at 105

degrees, her parents rushed her to the hospital. As she lay delirious, she heard the doctor tell them, "The infection has gone to the bone. If we cut out the infected portion of the heel, I think we can save the leg."

The problem, the doctor explained, stemmed from a cut on her foot that had become infected. With no sensation in her feet, Brenda had not felt the pain that would have signaled life-threatening infection.

As she was wheeled off to surgery, her nausea turned to fear. *Please, not my leg,* she prayed.

The moment she awoke from the anesthetic, she groped for her calf. "It's all right, Bren," her mother reassured her. "You still have your leg."

Surviving the series of operations that were required to fight the infection over the next three years took every ounce of Brenda's strength. When at last she blasted out into the sunlight soon after her 17th birthday, she was too busy catching up with life to think about swimming.

Bent on blending in, Brenda vaulted into adulthood, bypassing college and landing a computer-graphics job at a large engineering firm. She married and began climbing the corporate ladder.

And yet, something made Brenda keep swimming. Perhaps it was the pang she felt when her Uncle Mel suffered a stroke and began looking to her as his role model.

"All I have to do," he told her, as he struggled to adjust to a wheelchair, "is think about what you did as a kid, in that pool."

"Oh, that was years ago," she insisted. But each time she entered the water, she became that kid again, pushing herself to the limit.

"You're wasting your time with me," urged Frank Braxton, a friend from church she had corralled into doing laps with her. "You need to get into some real competition."

"And be the only disabled swimmer on the team? I've been there, and it's no fun," she insisted. "No racing

for me, ever again!" But on a May afternoon in 1987, a stranger's challenge changed everything.

When Paul McDowell spotted Brenda on the sidelines of a wheelchair-racing demonstration sponsored by the club her Uncle Mel had joined, he saw in her eyes the intensity of a serious athlete. Wheeling toward her, he said, "You're dying to try it, aren't you?"

In the 25 years since an auto accident had put him into a wheelchair, Paul McDowell had competed in national marathons and trained dozens of road racers. He could spot winners early on.

"All right," she said, "just once."

Brenda Smith
Paralympic medalist for the United States team in Barcelona, 1992

She swung into the chair, touched the wheels, and the lightweight racer sailed across the pavement. Deftly she maneuvered, lost in the sensation of speed, of control, of the power of her arm muscles over the rubber and steel beneath her. But when she wheeled back to McDowell, she said, "That's it for me!"

"Oh no, it's not," he shot back. "It's just the beginning!"

That winter Brenda's deteriorating leg muscles and knee joints forced her into the hospital for surgery. Flat on her back, she felt the inevitable closing in. For years she had fought doctors who tried to tell her that braces were putting too much strain on her legs and accelerating the muscular deterioration associated with spina bifida. Nothing, she insisted, would be worse than life in a wheelchair.

Now she saw that she no longer had a choice. But in her mind's eye, she also saw Paul McDowell proving that people in wheelchairs didn't have to wither away.

In the spring of 1988, 30-year-old Brenda entered her first wheelchair race and brought home a trophy.

In the spring of 1988, 30-year-old Brenda entered her first wheelchair race and brought home a trophy. When she joined an organization for disabled athletes called the Achilles Track Club, McDowell was the first person she saw. He greeted her news with an "I told you so" grin.

With McDowell's encouragement, Brenda began a vigorous training regimen. Soon she was turning heads at marathons by beating veteran wheelchair athletes. "If you keep on the way you're going, you could be in the Paralympics someday," he told her in the spring of 1991.

"The what?"

"It's the world's top competition for elite athletes with physical disabilities," he explained. Begun in 1960 in Rome with athletes who'd had spinal-cord injuries, it had expanded to include elite-level athletes with other physical disabilities.

"The next one is in Barcelona right after the Olympics. There'll be about 4,000 athletes competing."

"What do I have to do to get there?" Brenda asked.

"Let's take it one step at a time," he cautioned. "First there's the Southwest Regional meet you're competing in next month, in Arlington, Texas. People from all over the country will be there working toward spots on the U.S. Paralympic teams."

The number of Paralympic qualifying steps on McDowell's list was long, and the caliber of competition, daunting. Paralympic athletes were grouped into categories, according to their level of physical function. Competition would be fierce. "Many of these people work out full time," McDowell explained.

"Well, I work full time," Brenda said. "To make any kind of showing, I'll have to step up my evening swim workout."

So *that* explained Brenda's explosive power in the wheelchair. "You're a swimmer too?" McDowell asked.

"Swimming's from another lifetime. No big deal."

"It is a big deal. I want you to start gearing up for the swimming events in Arlington."

The Texas meet was a revelation. While Brenda performed well in the wheelchair competition, she blew the swimmers out of the water, beating every freestyler in her category. "These times are phenomenal," McDowell said. "You've got a serious shot at the U.S. Paralympic swim team."

McDowell began prodding her relentlessly. "You're being totally unrealistic, Brenda, thinking you can double-sport in Barcelona. You'll be up against talent far beyond anything you've seen so far. By rights, you should have begun elite-level training in a single sport years ago."

That could only mean swimming, the sport she associated as much with humiliation as with reward. "I need to do some thinking," she said.

Into the fall she trained with McDowell, perfecting her wheelchair technique, while training at the pool on her own. Also watching Brenda's development was fitness trainer Evan Brody at the club where she did her weight training.

"What you've been doing so far is about one-sixth of what a Paralympic-level athlete ought to be doing," he told her one morning in February. "You can't go much further on sheer talent. And you need to focus on one sport."

As Brenda listened, she realized that McDowell had been right. With the Paralympics only six months away, it was time to forget road racing, hire a swim coach and throw herself into her childhood dream.

Brody and his colleague Karen Sanders proposed a tightly controlled diet and exercise regimen. "Normally, it takes three years to peak as an Olympic-level athlete," Brody explained. "By training all at once, around your full-time work schedule, we run the risk that even if you bulk up, you'll start slowing down in the pool. Or you'll speed up, but damage your muscles in the process. You want to think it over?"

"It's now or never," Brenda answered. "I've got to go for it."

Working with Brenda's swim coach, Terry Kominski, Brody set out to pull the absolute maximum from Brenda's muscles. To measure her "maximal aerobic capacity"—the efficiency with which her muscle cells extracted oxygen from the blood—Brody and Sanders put her through the "VO2 max" tests. The results stunned them. "You're off the scale in terms of speed and endurance for female wheelchair athletes," Sanders told her. "In fact, these numbers are at the high end of the scale for males."

"The vast majority of athletes can train their whole lives and never get as much out of their muscles as you can," said Brody. "You've got a physiology most people would kill for!"

Brenda looked at Brody and Sanders, trying to absorb what they were telling her. There was no mistaking the look of awe on their faces. For the first time in her life, Brenda felt she could realize her childhood dream.

Many nights, when she dragged herself to her car after swim practice, she thought of what the numbers meant.

But there were days when she was so exhausted that even this wasn't enough to keep her going.

Why am I doing this to myself? she scribbled in her training log more than once. Each time, though, someone was there to remind her—her parents, her swim coach, her supervisors at work.

And always, there was her Uncle Mel, in failing health following a second stroke, calling late at night, giving her status reports on his efforts to help raise the $5,000 for her trip to Barcelona. "I won't be there to see you win your medal," he told her, "but I believed in you from Day One, and I'll be with you all the way."

On many days through the spring and early summer, Barcelona seemed far off indeed. Brenda and her husband had separated. Then her beloved Uncle Mel died. But through it all, Brenda never considered giving up.

Over the next couple of months, Brenda dropped 11 seconds from her 100-meter-backstroke time and six seconds from her 100-meter freestyle. "You're ready," Brody said finally when Brenda won five gold medals in July at the National Swimming Finals in Atlanta. "You were born to race, and you're going to do it."

On a hilltop overlooking Barcelona, the Paralympic torch glowed against the night sky. Sitting with Evan Brody just outside the Paralympic Village, Brenda was lost in thought. It was September 6, 1992. She was about to race for the medal she had dreamed of all her life, and her stomach was churning.

Brenda's classification—an eight out of ten—was going to pit her against swimmers with enough use of their legs to be able to dive off the blocks, a tremendous advantage when victories are measured in hundredths of a second. Her physiological testing had overclassified her, but nothing could be done about it.

From her pocket, Brenda pulled a computer printout listing the records of the swimmers in her category.

> "You're ready,"
> Brody said finally . . .
> "You were born to
> race, and you're
> going to do it."

"Look at these times, Evan," she burst out. "Priya Cooper from Australia, a full second ahead of me going in, and she's 17—half my age! The German woman, Britta Siegers, and Rebeccah Bornemann, from Canada. I'll be the only one starting in the water. How can I possibly compensate for the edge the others get from a diving start?"

"You're going to do what you've always had to do," Brody said. "And that's to be just a little bit better, a little bit faster."

> Brenda knew she had swum faster than ever before.

Brenda tensed for the signal that would begin the 50-meter freestyle. Behind her, the seven other women took their places on the blocks as she clung to the wall.

All my life, I've had to be just a little faster, she repeated.

At the starting signal Brenda shot forward.

Oblivious to the noise of the crowd, she dissolved into an arc of muscle, speed and grace. Stroke by stroke, she gained on the pack. She was on Bornemann's shoulder, then neck and neck. Slowly she pulled ahead of the Canadian, still behind Cooper, and nearly even with Siegers.

In a final lunge, she touched the wall, surfaced a hairsbreadth behind Siegers and turned to watch the numbers light up on the board: 0:36:60. Brenda knew she had swum faster than ever before. Only .22 seconds behind silver medalist Britta Siegers, she had won the bronze. She had done her country proud. "Representing the United States of America . . ." the announcer boomed as Brenda approached the podium to receive her medal. Her eyes gleamed, and she wore the smile of a little girl, now a woman, born to race.

In addition to this individual triumph, Brenda also won a gold medal as a member of the 100-meter freestyle relay team.

THE HORSE NOBODY WANTED

by Jay Hovdey

To almost everyone Sunday Silence looked like a losing bet. But Charlie Whittingham saw the racehorse inside the rogue.

A HUSH fell over the crowd at Hollywood Park as the auctioneer begged for one last bid. On a raised platform, a black thoroughbred with a squiggle of white running down his face pawed nervously at the floor. A few coughs fluttered up from the crowd, but nothing more.

Down went the auctioneer's hammer, and the colt was led out of the sales ring. His owner, Arthur Hancock, had set a minimum price of $50,000, but the bidding had topped out at $32,000.

It was March 1988, and the black colt, named Sunday Silence, had just become a two-time loser in the market-place — first at a Kentucky sale and now at California's top thoroughbred auction. Shaking his head, Hancock loaded the horse into a van for the trip back to

Kentucky. En route, the driver suffered a heart attack and the van tumbled off a Texas highway. A local veterinarian patched up the horse and sent him home two weeks later.

Not long after, Charles Edward Whittingham met Sunday Silence for the first time. At age 75, Charlie Whittingham was the dean of America's thoroughbred racehorse trainers. He sported a personality that was one part charm, one part wise old sage and one part redneck. He had begun training racehorses during the Great Depression, when a third-place finish meant enough pocket money to put beans in the belly and a little honey in the mash. Whittingham won, or went hungry. So he won. And he came through it all with a flint-hard attitude that put work first and everything else a distant second. "Sleep's overrated," Whittingham once said upon a 4 A.M. arrival at the track to begin his workday. "You get all the sleep you need after you die."

After Sunday Silence failed to sell, Hancock had offered his longtime friend Whittingham a half-interest in the colt for $25,000. Whittingham took the deal, sight unseen. Now, as the trainer finally beheld his purchase, he was less than impressed.

Sunday Silence stared at the world with the hardened eye of a juvenile delinquent. His hocks — the elbowlike joints hinging the lower part of the back legs — almost scraped together as he walked. He was light on muscle in the back end, and his chest was deep but narrow. Whittingham searched for something good to say. "Sometimes they surprise you," he offered. "Let's see what he looks like after we've had him a while."

"Sunday, Stop It!" Soon Sunday Silence began training for a racing career in Southern California. From the start, he was willful and uncompromising, always full of vinegar, whether in his stall or exercising on the track. Each morning at dawn, the colt would buck and rear as Whittingham's horses waited for the training grounds to open. In a crowd of 40 horses he became a liability, even a danger. He seemed to be some kind of throw-

back to the days when horses were hunted, and fear and hunger ruled their lives.

Pam Mabes, Sunday Silence's exercise rider, tried to follow Whittingham's prescribed routine: a walk, then a jog, then a gallop. This was too polite for Sunday Silence. He would prance and buck instead of walking. Mabes would fight for control until Whittingham yelled, "Just let him go!" Then with a burst of energy, Sunday Silence would leave his well-mannered stablemates in the dust. "Charlie, are you sure you don't want somebody else on this horse?" Mabes once pleaded. "To tell you the truth, I'm kind of afraid of him."

"Naw, girl, you're doing just fine," Whittingham replied with half a smile. "Don't fight him. Just go with him."

Mabes soon discovered that the key was keeping Sunday Silence in constant motion. He could never stand completely still. What he wanted to do was run — as fast as he could. The harder he worked, the better he acted. When Mabes geared down, he would protest by dipping his head between his legs and bucking to a stop. "Sunday, stop it!" she'd cry, nearly flying out of the saddle. Soon, everyone around the barn began referring to the colt as "Sunday Stop It!"

Whittingham allowed Sunday Silence special latitude. He reminded his crew to be patient, firm and kind. This one, he told them, could be worth the trouble.

All the while, Whittingham was cultivating the race-horse inside the rogue. After six decades in the company of thoroughbreds, he could recognize raw potential behind physical defects or mental immaturity. Whittingham allowed Sunday Silence special latitude. He reminded his crew to be patient, firm and kind. This one, he told them, could be worth the trouble.

Even before Sunday Silence made his first start, though, across the country on the East Coast a robust colt with a rich caramel coat had emerged to win two major stakes races at New York's Belmont Park. As racing's heir apparent, he was treated like a king. Even his name — Easy Goer — sounded like a winner. By the end of 1988, Easy Goer was a heavy favorite in the early betting for the 1989 Kentucky Derby.

Sunday Silence, on the other hand, was barely a blip on the West Coast radar. He lost his first race, won his next, and then finished second in his final start of 1988. There were no major headlines and no fan clubs, but that was just fine with Whittingham.

On March 2, 1989, Sunday Silence dispatched six undistinguished opponents in his first race of the new year. After another victory, Hancock received a flood of offers for his share of Sunday Silence. "What do you think I should do, Charlie?" Hancock asked his partner.

"Do whatever you want," Whittingham said. "Anything could happen to the horse between now and his next race. They're like fresh strawberries — they can spoil overnight."

Natural Rivals. On April 8, 1989, in the space of an hour and a half, two bombshells landed squarely at the nerve center of horse racing. At 4:15 P.M. at Aqueduct Race Course on Long Island, Easy Goer made a shambles of his competition in the Gotham Stakes. Thirteen lengths ahead of his closest opponent, his time for the mile distance came within a blink of the long-standing American record.

Easy Goer was barely bedded down in his stall when, 3,000 miles away, Sunday Silence pranced into the saddling paddock to prepare for the Santa Anita Derby. When asked by a reporter for his reaction to Easy Goer's triumph, Whittingham paused to praise him. But then he added a word of caution. "The last time I checked," he said, "the Kentucky Derby was a mile and a quarter."

Twenty minutes later, Sunday Silence won the Santa Anita Derby by 11 lengths, running the 1⅛-mile course with an abandon that suggested the Kentucky Derby distance would be no problem at all. Suddenly, American horse racing had its greatest rivalry in years: Sunday Silence of the West Coast would run against Easy Goer of the East Coast. With the race now only a month away, no one could remember a Kentucky Derby in which sentiment was so clearly divided along geographic lines.

Anxious Waiting. When Easy Goer arrived at Churchill Downs outside Louisville, Ky., soon after Sunday Silence, it set up a Derby week rife with contrasts. If Easy Goer was leading-man handsome, Sunday Silence was the beguiling bad boy. He had attained a full-chested, well-muscled masculinity, with a certain swagger to go along with his height. But the racing press banged the drum loudly for Easy Goer — and trumpeted his impending coronation as the next Secretariat.

In the meantime, Arthur Hancock was being bombarded with offers to sell part of Sunday Silence. "One guy wants to buy a quarter interest for $500,000," Hancock told Whittingham. "How about I put up 12½ percent of my share and you do the same?"

Whittingham's response was immediate. "I'm not selling!" he shot back.

But Hancock's butterflies didn't disappear. On the morning that entries were taken for the Derby, he watched Sunday Silence in a half-mile workout. Whittingham clicked off his stopwatch as the colt glided to a halt. Hancock waited anxiously for an evaluation. Just right? A bit too fast? "C'mon, Charlie," he asked. "What's the word?"

"We will get the money," Whittingham said calmly.

Hancock blinked hard against the chilly wind. "What are you saying, Charlie? How can you —"

"My boy," Whittingham interrupted with a twinkle in his eye, "we will get the money."

Pressure Cooker. Despite the 40-degree chill and drizzly rain, almost 123,000 people turned out for the Derby showdown between Sunday Silence and Easy Goer on May 6, 1989.

The celebrities watching the race from the lofty heights of Millionaire's Row and the mere mortals cramming the huge track grandstand expected a horse race for the ages. They also expected Easy Goer to win. Of the nearly $30 million bet on the Derby across America, the bulk of it was on Easy Goer's handsome head.

On the face of it, the odds made sense. Easy Goer seemed mature beyond his years. With each victory, he impressed more and more observers with his graceful stride and relentless acceleration.

Sunday Silence, on the other hand, remained a question mark. With only six races in his life, was he seasoned enough to challenge Easy Goer? Could Sunday Silence behave himself in the Derby pressure cooker, which could rattle even the calmest racehorse?

The black colt was all eyes and ears as his groom, Charles Clay, led him to the saddling paddock. Sunday Silence's blood was boiling beneath his skin, but he kept his head. Then, as the contestants proceeded toward the starting gate, one lost a horseshoe, necessitating a nine-minute delay. Could Sunday Silence cope with the unexpected inactivity? When jockey Pat Valenzuela dismounted briefly, Sunday Silence stood still, intent on the job at hand like an old pro.

Finally, at 5:42 P.M. the field of 15 three-year-old thoroughbreds spilled out of the starting gate. Sunday Silence was expected to be in front of Easy Goer through the early stages of the race. And there he was, tracking the pace-setters as they thundered past the stands and began the journey around the first turn and down the long backstretch. Easy Goer, saving his best for last, galloped along in the middle of the herd.

With only six races in his life, was he seasoned enough to challenge Easy Goer? Could Sunday Silence behave himself in the Derby pressure cooker . . .

As the leaders approached the distant turn, still nearly a half-mile from the finish, Easy Goer began to make up ground on his rival. Pat Day, the hometown hero riding Easy Goer, knew Churchill Downs like the back of his hand. Day shook his reins and asked for more run.

Suddenly, Sunday Silence ignited a spark of hidden energy and spurted away, putting several yards between him and his rival. Unfazed, Easy Goer continued to pound the muddy ground, as Day kept Sunday Silence's black tail squarely in his sights.

The final quarter-mile of the Derby is all straightaway, affording horses an honest chance to win the race if they are good enough. Sunday Silence still had an advantage of three lengths — maybe 25 feet — over Easy Goer. But Easy Goer could gobble up three lengths in a few strides.

Then, a strange fandango ensued. Spooked by the noisy crowd and startled by Valenzuela's whip, Sunday Silence swerved to the left, then to the right, then left again. In the stands, Whittingham screamed in vain for Valenzuela to sheathe the whip and steer with his hands. It was a nightmare in the making. Sunday Silence seemed to have had the race won. Now he was trying to give it away.

Day angled Easy Goer to the left and began riding with all his strength, while up ahead Valenzuela was still fighting Sunday Silence for control. With 150 yards to run, Easy Goer's fans thought they had a chance. Then, in a flash, the finish line arrived. Erratic to the end, Sunday Silence sailed past the white winning post 2½ lengths clear of his rival.

As a beaming Valenzuela brought Sunday Silence to a stop and headed for the winner's stand, Whittingham was mobbed by family and friends. Chants of "Charlie! Charlie!" echoed through the crowd as he and Hancock went down to the track.

A track attendant stepped up with the traditional Derby blanket of red roses and draped it over the winner's neck. Whittingham and Hancock each took a long, appreciative look at Sunday Silence. This horse of theirs, this misbehaving reject of a thoroughbred, had just won the world's most important race.

Sunday Silence and Easy Goer faced each other three more times before the end of their careers. First, Sunday Silence narrowly beat Easy Goer in Baltimore's Preakness Stakes. Then Easy Goer thwarted Sunday Silence's bid for the Triple Crown, winning New York's Belmont Stakes. Their final showdown took place on November 4, 1989, in the world's richest race, the $3-million Breeders' Cup Classic. Once more, bettors made Easy Goer the favorite. And for one final, decisive time, Sunday Silence beat him.

THE YOUNG WOMAN AND THE SEA

by Priscilla Buckley

**Against heavy odds, French heroine
Florence Arthaud blazed a new chapter
in the annals of transatlantic sailing.**

A SINGLE SAILOR at her helm, the giant gold trimaran shot out of the ocean haze on August 3, 1990, touched down on the rocky shores of Lizard Point and made history. From New York harbor to England's southernmost point, she had traversed the Atlantic in nine days, 21 hours and 42 minutes, pulverizing the existing record for a solo crossing by 38 hours.

For the skipper, the crossing represented nine days of clambering between the trimaran's three hulls on nets as the boat bucked wildly on white-capped seas; nine days of wrestling with winches and sails in storms raging with 40-knot winds; nine days of sleep in half-hour bouts, an eternity of relentless vigilance and mind-bending solitude. Few men are capable of enduring such an ordeal, and that made the feat all the more stunning. The skipper

was not a man, but a high-voltage, chestnut-haired wisp of a woman named Florence Arthaud.

At 33, Florence is considered one of the best sailors in the world. "She's the first woman who dared take on the men," says fellow navigator Bruno Peyron, whose transatlantic crossing record she shattered. "And she's the only one capable of competing at the level she does today."

In her native France, Florence, with her irresistible smile, has become a national heroine, gracing magazine covers and breaking television viewing records. Yet her success has rubbed some people the wrong way. That a woman should have dominated the sports press during the crossing and then gone on to shatter the record was more than some could gracefully bear. Worse yet, she had not intended to try for a record. "I simply wanted to get to know my boat in preparation for the Route du Rhum in November," she explains. "This is the kind of experience you need to win. But first and foremost, you have to love the ocean."

Love of the ocean has been a tradition in the Arthaud family. Florence's father ran Editions Arthaud, a publishing house specializing in books evoking adventures in mountains, deserts — and oceans. Legendary navigators, including Eric Tabarly, a national hero for having won the single-handed transatlantic race from Plymouth (Britain) to Newport (United States) in 1964, came to the family home in Paris to dine with their publisher. "We listened to my father's authors talk about their adventures," recalls Florence. "They filled my head with dreams."

Sports were encouraged in the family. Florence and her two brothers spent winters on the ski slopes, summers swimming, water-skiing and sailing. It was, she says, "a perfect childhood." But as an adolescent Florence developed a passion for fast boats and cars. When she was 17, a serious car accident left her in a coma. She spent a month and a half in the hospital recovering from two skull fractures and partial facial paralysis, and was left with spinal injuries that would plague her for life. Yet even that did not slow her down.

In 1976 Florence flew to Newport to watch Tabarly win the single-handed Plymouth–Newport again. For the return trip she joined Jean-Claude Parisis on his boat — her first transatlantic sail. It was the turning point in her life. "From then on," she says, "I was obsessed with one thing: crossing the Atlantic again."

As an 18-year-old medical student, Florence spent more time on the water than in lecture halls. Her parents protested. Florence persisted. When yet again they forbade her to sail, Florence left home for good. "Only the ocean could give me the freedom, adventure and solitude I needed," she says.

On November 5, 1978, at age 21, Florence entered the Route du Rhum, her first solo transatlantic race. It is a grueling 3,600-mile crossing from Saint-Malo on

France's northern coast to the shores of Guadeloupe. "I had chosen my boat because it was safe, not fast," Florence explains. "I knew I couldn't win, but all I wanted was not to look ridiculous." Three and a half weeks later, she sailed into the Pointe-Ö-Pitre harbor, a respectable 11th out of 40.

Over the next decade Florence racked up ten transatlantic races. Each time the prodigious 5-foot, 3-inch, 120-pound dynamo learned more about herself. "At first I thought eating and sleeping were a waste of time," she recalls, "and all my mistakes were the result of being exhausted. I had to learn my body's rhythms, to know how little I could sleep and still maintain myself intellectually."

Soon Florence won the respect of the sailing community. "Florence is an exceptional helmsman," says navigator Alain Gabbay. "She goes very fast and is afraid of nothing." From among her rivals she gained a number of admirers, and ultimately friends: past winners of the Route du Rhum Frenchman Philippe Poupon and Canadian Mike Birch, as well as her idol, Eric Tabarly.

Yet along with the fulfillment of being at sea came financial anxieties. She was the top woman in the circuit, but she rarely broke the top ten. Sponsors came and went, and without constant financial backing, Florence had to rent or buy run-down or ill-adapted boats. Yet, though hopelessly handicapped by her equipment, she had the nagging feeling her worst enemy was herself. She pushed her boats and herself too hard.

Florence was close to quitting. "I was sick of traipsing from office to office, dinner to dinner in Paris trying to find financing. I wanted the means to *win*." Then, in 1988, the miracle happened. Christian Garrel, the chairman and CEO of Pierre 1er, a Paris-based real-estate firm, summoned Florence to his office. Fifteen minutes later she left with a commitment of 50 million francs over five years, enough to design and construct a state-of-the-art boat and pay for a seven-man support team.

In September 1988 Florence's trimaran, *Pierre 1er*, began to take shape. In the ACX shipyards in Brest, workers constructed the boat's curved crossbeams and a towering 90-foot wing-mast of high-modulus carbon fiber, originally used in the aeronautics industry. Simultaneously, in the JTA shipyard in Nantes, the 60-foot central hull and its flanking floats were molded of carbon fiber and foam.

The components were then shipped to an atelier outside Paris. There the compact cabin was filled with essential technological wizardry: three automatic pilots; radar; the GPS, which with the help of a satellite connection establishes the real position of the boat; and an instrument measuring the angle and speed of the wind and boat. Finally there was the routing equipment: a computer with a program providing, among other things, nautical maps and the boat's position on them, route and wind-speed calculations and the telex, with which Florence communicates with her Paris-based router, meteorologist Louis Bodin.

During a race Bodin's function is to help Florence find the fastest route from start to finish. He collects and evaluates meteorological forecasts, and feeds this and other data into a computer, which calculates theoretically optimal routes. Each time the weather changes or new forecasts become available, everything must be reevaluated and discussed either by radio or telex with Florence, who makes the final decision.

It was on the return trip that Florence, alone at the helm, shattered the world record.

On the evening of March 28, 1990, the *Pierre 1er*, with her golden mast and hulls, was christened on the River Seine in Paris. The next few months of trial testing aimed at perfecting the trimaran in time for the Route du Rhum in November. For her maiden transatlantic voyage, Florence and Patrick Maurel entered her in the June Twostar race from Plymouth to Newport and finished third. It was on the return trip that Florence, alone at the helm, shattered the world record.

In September Florence's old spinal injuries landed her in a surgical collar and cut dead her training. Her doctors advised her to forgo the Route du Rhum, that it was too dangerous. But Florence refused. She had dreamed of winning the race for too long.

November 4, 1990. Starting day, Saint-Malo. All the sailing greats — Philippe Poupon, Mike Birch — were there, in top condition and with superb trimarans, and tens of thousands of spectators saw them off. Florence made a good start and began regaining her strength. After just a couple of days, she tossed her collar to the Atlantic.

With the wind blowing at 55 knots, four navigators were forced to abandon the race within the first 48 hours. But Florence kept her head and sailed prudently. When she wasn't heaving winches and lashing down sails, she tracked her progress on illuminated screens in the cabin, snacked on powdered soups and pasta, and napped fitfully to the constant battering of the waves. By November 7th she had covered 1,000 miles and learned she was in the lead.

From the beginning, one disaster after another befell her. The meteorological-map decoder stopped working on the third day. Next the instrument panel broke off and crucial instruments went dead, including two automatic pilots and the radio and telex connecting her with Louis Bodin: Florence was cut off from the outside world and had nothing to rely on but her own experience and intuition. For two days she was confronted with highly treacherous weather conditions. Then a fuel leak forced her to use the last working automatic pilot only sporadically. She would now have to stay at the helm 20 hours a day. "I've got no luck," she wrote in her log, verging on despair. "But I must hold on: 1,800 miles to go."

In the midst of these difficulties, the worst trial of all struck. Florence began hemorrhaging profusely on and off for three days. Too weak to walk, she was a breath away from releasing her distress buoy — an automatic forfeit. But then she figured that by the time help arrived, it would be too late. *Besides, I've never abandoned a race in my life,* she said to herself, *and I'm not going to start now.*

Trembling with weakness on the tenth day, Florence turned her bow to the wind and, despite the pressures of competition, slept deeply for three hours. That night, with no means to illuminate her compass, she steered by the stars, and suddenly it was an epiphany. The sky, the sea, the stars: They existed for her alone. Never had her boat seemed so noble, nor the movement of the waves so comforting. "I was alone with God," she remembers. "With each falling star I made a wish: 'God, sustain the wind!' 'God, help me win!'"

In perfect symbiosis she and her boat surged onward. Other contenders became mired in the stillness of an anticyclone. Florence skirted it to the south and, with the wind behind her, sailed directly for Guadeloupe. Early on the fifteenth day, November 18, a plane swooped down low over the *Pierre ler* to give her the good news. She was 60 miles ahead of second-place Mike Birch.

Later that morning, the sight of Guadeloupe left Florence giddy with emotion. Soon the first boats came out to greet her. As dry-lipped and hollow-eyed Florence made the obligatory circuit of the island, they grew in number. By the time she entered the Pointe-à-Pitre harbor, she was escorted by hundreds of craft trailing banners and sounding foghorns.

Tens of thousands of spectators jammed the piers before her. When she finally crossed the finish line, fireworks exploded, and she was besieged by joyful family, teammates and friends. Not only was she the first woman to win a transatlantic race, but her time of 14 days, ten hours and eight minutes had blazed a new Route du Rhum record. And this despite all the handicaps. Or perhaps because of them. For they had forced her to slow down, to control herself, as she put it, "to be reasonable for once."

A telegram was waiting from Eric Tabarly: "It was the victory of a sailor." Not a woman. Not a media darling. Louis le Pensec, the French Minister of Overseas Departments and Territories, presented her with a cup and a message from President François Mitterrand: "You have triumphed over the elements, technical and physical problems, as well as some people's skepticism." Through the haze of emotion and fatigue, vindication was far from Florence's mind. All she could think was, *I am proud of myself, and life is beautiful.*

UNFORGETTABLE JIM VALVANO

by Dick Vitale

A friend recalls the man who lived the motto, "Don't give up. Don't ever give up."

JIM VALVANO was one of those rare people who could light up a room just by walking into it. I first met him when we were both coaching college basketball. After being fired by the NBA Detroit Pistons in 1979, I ended up broadcasting games on TV. So did Jimmy. But along the way he achieved coaching honors the rest of us could only dream about. He was the most brilliant, energetic and inspirational man I've ever known.

He was also the funniest. Good-natured teasing had always been part of our friendship. ("Dickie V at my alma mater!" he said when I told him I'd become an assistant at Rutgers. "There goes the value of my degree!") And he delighted in pranks. One time, he and John Saunders, the anchorman and one of Jimmy's closest friends on our ESPN broadcast team, were dancing a little shuffle together during a commercial break, just for fun. They talked me into joining in, and the producer said, "Why don't you guys dance as we come back to you live?" So we begin dancing, the camera comes back, and those two cut out — leaving me dancing alone like an idiot!

Jim could be surprisingly crafty in his humor, as I learned in 1988 when I was the "guest of honor" at a roast. Jimmy, then the head coach at North Carolina State, was doing a pretty good job of poking fun at me. He mentioned my miserable coaching record with the Pistons, my looks — even my bald head. But he hadn't touched my deepest secret, one I thought I'd kept from him for years: I, too, had applied for the N.C. State job — and lost out to him.

Now, just as it appeared Jim had finished his lighthearted put-downs, he set me up for the biggest. "I have something I want to display here about your man Dickie V," he told the crowd. He took a letter from his pocket and started reading: "Dear Dick, We are sorry to inform you that we have named Jim Valvano head coach at North Carolina State. . . ."

I thought nobody knew about that letter. Jimmy had apparently saved it for years, just waiting. I didn't know how to react, but then the crowd's laughter became so loud that Jimmy couldn't even finish. In the short but wonderfully rich history of "Jimmy V" capers, this was a classic.

Humor, though, was just part of Jimmy's personality. He had a way of making everyone feel comfortable with him. One night the two of us went out to eat with Bill Cosby after we had appeared on his show. At dinner, Jimmy had Cosby — one of the funniest men in America — laughing so hard he could barely eat.

"No Reason We Can't" James Thomas Valvano was born in New York City into a close-knit, emotional family. All four of his grandparents had come from Naples, Italy. His maternal grandfather was James Vitale — no relation of mine, despite the name. But Jimmy didn't pronounce it Vi-TAL, as I did. "Say your name Vi-TAL-ee," he told me.

He gave it to me with characteristic enthusiasm. "Be proud, *paisan*. Be proud you're Italian."

Jimmy's first love was basketball. Early on, he decided he would become a coach, and he plotted his career on index cards, in five-year increments. His timetable proved stunningly conservative.

He started as an assistant coach the year he graduated from Rutgers, and by age 23 he was head coach at Johns Hopkins, which hadn't had a winning season in nearly a quarter century. In Jimmy's first year, they won ten and lost nine. He went on to Bucknell, and then to Iona — a small Catholic school in the New York City suburbs with a mediocre basketball program.

> *At Iona, Jimmy showed an almost magical ability to get the most out of his players.*

At Iona, Jimmy showed an almost magical ability to get the most out of his players. He hugged them as they came off the court; he yelled encouragement. He would even bench his star player as a reminder that they were a *team*. He cajoled them, made them believe they could do anything they set their minds to — even beat a top team like Louisville in Madison Square Garden. "There's no reason we can't!" Jimmy said, and his players went out and did it.

Jim was a master at controlling the tempo of a game. His teams would confuse rivals by slowing down against fast-paced opponents, or running all-out against teams that expected a slow game. He showed an uncanny knack for making substitutions — bringing in a player who would instantly do well. In five years he led the Iona Gaels to a 95–46 record and two National Collegiate Athletic Association (NCAA) tournament appearances.

David Against Goliath. In 1980, when Jim was only 34, North Carolina State beckoned. He took his new state by storm, becoming a round-the-clock salesman using every angle — booster clubs, appearances on talk shows, fast-food commercials, the whole shebang — to attract the best high-school players in the country to his Wolfpack teams.

In a short time, his efforts paid off. Against all odds, N.C. State beat North Carolina and Virginia to reach the 1983 NCAA tournament. All through the playoffs, Jimmy kept telling his players: "We belong here. We can win this thing. Don't give up!"

Game after game, the Wolfpack advanced in dramatic fashion. Fans around the country watched as the team made it all the way to Albuquerque, N.M., for the finals against the University of Houston.

Houston, one of the greatest college teams of all time, had lost only two games out of 33 all season. N.C. State, in contrast, had lost ten of 35. Reporters thought the game was a real M&M'er — a mismatch. "Rain would make it perfect," wrote one. "It always rains at executions."

Following Jimmy's game plan perfectly, State took an early lead. He instructed his players to keep the ball away from Houston's big, intimidating dunkers, Akeem (now Hakeem) Olajuwon and Clyde Drexler. At halftime, the Wolfpack led by eight. Jimmy addressed his team: "You will never, ever, for the rest of your life in whatever field you go into, have the emotion and feeling you will have when the final buzzer goes off and we win."

But Houston came out strong, and the second half was pure Maalox time. With the score tied, State hit a shot at the final buzzer. The Wolfpack had won, 54–52. National champs! Jimmy was right where he wanted to be, at the pinnacle of his profession. When a reporter asked him about Albuquerque, Jimmy said, "Albuquerque is the greatest city the Lord ever made. My wife is going to be pregnant — she doesn't know this yet — and I'm going to name the kid Al B. Querque!"

"V and V." Jimmy went on to guide his teams to two conference titles and seven NCAA tournament appearances. But in 1989 a dark cloud appeared on the horizon — a book alleged that the N.C. State program had violated a number of NCAA rules.

A grueling investigation cleared Jimmy of any personal wrongdoing and found only three violations by the team.

Still, N.C. State was placed on two years' probation, and the school felt it could not move beyond the controversy as long as Valvano remained.

It was a traumatic time for Jimmy. After reaching a settlement with the school, he received lucrative coaching offers but decided to go into television instead. No amount of money or fame was worth what he had been through.

There was another reason, too. Going all-out to be the best at his profession, he had become so occupied with wins and losses he didn't have the time at home he wanted. "I remember one Father's Day when I happened to be home, and nobody had planned anything," he told a reporter once. "How could they? I'd probably never been home on Father's Day before. I might've been in Atlanta giving a Father's Day speech or in Chicago receiving a Father of the Year award, but you can bet I wasn't home."

That would change now. Jim suddenly had time for dinners alone with his wife, Pam, time to spend with his daughters, Lee Ann, 11, Jamie, 19, and Nicole, 22.

And so Jim and I became partners broadcasting games for ESPN and ABC. "V and V," our fans called us. I never saw anyone take to television more naturally than Jimmy. His knowledge of the game and love of teaching blended beautifully on the air. As college basketball surged in popularity, our national exposure increased dramatically. Again Jimmy was riding high on life.

Award for Courage. One day in June 1992, I called Jimmy at home. He said he was awaiting the results of a physical. The doctor had ordered a spinal scan, thinking that pain in Jimmy's lower back might be from a disc problem.

But the image that came back showed something far worse — Jim's vertebrae were dark when they should have been white. "Doc, you forgot to use the flash," Jim quipped, hiding his fear.

"Coach," the doctor replied, "I'm 90-percent sure this is cancer." The test results confirmed it: bone cancer. Jimmy was 46 years old.

Jim Valvano
*(right) poses
with the author.*

He attacked the disease the only way he knew how — with all his energy. A magazine article once said of Jimmy: "If Vee liked a movie, he saw it five times. If Vee liked a song, he memorized it, sang it 20 times a day and talked his kids into singing it. Vee couldn't throw half or three-quarters of his heart into anything; he had to throw it all." While receiving chemotherapy, he read every book on cancer he could find. He'd spent a career telling players never to give up. Now he said it to himself every day.

He made his battle public, too, and wanted to keep working despite his illness. In our hotel room the night before an ESPN preseason planning meeting that October, he was taking painkillers like you wouldn't believe, to relieve what he described as a toothache running through his entire body. But the next day at the meeting, he was the same old feisty Jimmy.

He bore his pain so gracefully that it was easy for those around him to forget it. I once complained to him about my hectic schedule the next day. "Do you want to come with *me* tomorrow?" he replied. "You can drive me to chemotherapy, watch me throw up and see people faced with real adversity." That hit me like 5,000 pounds. Finally, he said something I'll never forget. "You're missing the important stuff, Dickie. You're moving too fast. You gotta slow it down, baby." I have a picture of him in my office, and I think of that time whenever I look at it.

At the American Sports Awards that March, I introduced Jimmy Valvano as winner of the Arthur Ashe Award for Courage. The cancer had advanced, and Jim thought he might not make the ceremony. But he came — in a wheelchair.

I was broken up as Duke University basketball coach Mike Krzyzewski, one of Jimmy's closest friends, and I helped him shuffle to the podium for his acceptance speech. He looked weak, his skin a pale olive color. Finally, he made it to the microphone. "That's the lowest I've seen Dick Vitale since the Detroit Pistons' owner told him he should go into broadcasting!"

The place went nuts. Twenty-four hours earlier, he could barely talk, and now he was cracking jokes.

When the laughter subsided, Jimmy drew from some final reserve of energy, deep in his heart, as if his life wouldn't be complete without sending out his message one last time.

To me there are three things everyone should do every day. Number one is laugh. You should laugh every day. Number two is think — spend some time in thought. Number three, you should have your emotions move you to tears. If you laugh, think and cry, that's a heck of a day.

Ralph Waldo Emerson said, "Nothing great was ever achieved without enthusiasm." I urge all of you to enjoy your life, to be enthusiastic every day. To keep your dreams alive in spite of your problems.

> *Jimmy drew from some final reserve of energy, deep in his heart, as if his life wouldn't be complete without sending out his message one last time.*

Now I look where I am and what I want to do. He
paused. *With ESPN's support, we are starting the Jimmy V
Foundation for cancer research. Its motto is "Don't give up.
Don't ever give up." That's what I'm going to try to do every
minute I have left. I will thank God for the day and the
moment I have.*

*I know I gotta go. But I have one last thing to say.
Cancer can take away all my physical abilities. It cannot
touch my mind, it cannot touch my heart and it cannot
touch my soul. And those three things are going to carry
on forever.*

On April 28, less than two months later, Jim Valvano
died with his wife and family at his bedside. The speech
he had given was played on a giant screen to the
Opening Day crowd at Yankee Stadium, where Jimmy
had hoped to throw out the first ball, and in other cities
around the country.

In the months that followed, Jimmy's speech rallied
support for cancer research and inspired thousands of
cancer victims, who heard the message Jimmy Valvano
had spent a career telling his players: *Don't give up. Don't
ever give up.*

THE HAPPINESS GAMES: WHERE EVERYONE WINS

by Charles Parmiter

Trying is what the Special Olympics is all about.

FOR ADRIANO PALESE, a shy, teenager from Italy with mental retardation, the trip to Glasgow for July 1989's six-day third European Summer Special Olympics Games was pure magic. He flew in a plane and glimpsed the Atlantic Ocean — both for the first time. He also heard his first bagpipes, saw his first kilt and marched in his first parade.

Adriano was so enthralled by these delights that he nearly forgot why he was in Scotland. Midway through the final of the 800-meter run, Adriano was blissfully loping along in last place, 50 meters behind the leaders, oblivious to the frantic urgings of his coach and teammates. *"Vai, vai,"* they screamed. "Go, go!" All to no avail, until an exasperated voice yelled in Italian from the sideline, "For God's sake, Adriano, at least *try!"*

The effect was electric. As if stung by a bee, Adriano suddenly unleashed a powerful spurt that propelled him past astonished rivals and across the finish line. Tears of joy streamed down his cheeks as officials draped a gold medal around his neck. "I did it! I did it!" he sobbed. "I tried!"

Trying is what the Special Olympics is all about. To one dismayed by the occasional drug scandals, commercialism and petty politics of the Olympic Games, the Special Olympics brought refreshing memories of the ideals these contests once embodied. Here winning was less important than effort, comradeship and respect. In the hard-fought basketball final, eventually won by

Yugoslavia over Greece, a Greek player collided with an opponent and crashed to the floor, writhing in agony. Ignoring the referee's signals to continue play, athletes from both teams clustered around the injured Greek, supporting his head and gently massaging his twisted ankle until he could walk again.

The sportsmanship of these athletes affected spectators as well. Fanoulla Alexandrou, a Cypriot, won the 15-meter unassisted swim in 22.91 seconds. But the loudest cheers were for Mary Theresa Brady, an Irish woman with extensive disabilities, who refused to quit and completed the course in 37.7 seconds. Her smile when she finally touched the end of the pool could have illuminated the Hall of Mirrors at Versailles. The athletes' marks at Glasgow might have been less than world class, but they set records of happiness.

The first Special Olympics Games were held in Chicago in 1968 — an outgrowth of an early 1960s summer camp for people with mental retardation — founded by Eunice Shriver, sister of the late U.S. president John F. Kennedy, in the backyard of her Maryland home. Her sister Rosemary has mental retardation; for Eunice the Special Olympics is a labor of love. Today Sargent Shriver, Eunice's husband, is chairman of Special Olympics International, the Washington based organization that runs the biennial world games and licenses the European version, held every few years.

Those 1968 "international" games drew 1,000 athletes from the United States and Canada. By contrast, the Glasgow event attracted 2,200 athletes from 31 European delegations, including (for the first time) those of the Soviet Union and the freshly "independent" states of Estonia, Lithuania and Latvia. Picked by local selection boards, the participants all had mental retardation, some with congenital physical disabilities as well. They competed in 13 events ranging from track and field to ten-pin bowling, and there were varying levels of competition to give everybody a chance.

The atmosphere in Glasgow was festive as a capacity

throng of 35,000 shoehorned into Celtic Park for the opening ceremonies. Drums rolled and bagpipes wailed as the athletes, nattily attired in their national colors, marched around the stadium. Flags waved, fireworks went off overhead and the Olympic flame whooshed skyward as the Duke of Edinburgh, patron of the events, pronounced the games open. Jordan's Queen Noor and Monaco's Prince Albert marched with the athletes, and a host of other celebrities were on hand.

Budgeted at 3.3 million pounds, the games coincided with Glasgow's celebrations as Europe's 1990 "City of Culture." Oddly, when executive director of the Glasgow Special Olympics Michael Dale approached the city's big businesses for contributions, they were reluctant. "I don't think they're ready for what we call cause-related activity," sighed Dale.

Glasgow's citizens, however, filled the gap. Firemen dropped out of the sky in parachutes to raise money; salespeople from a department store slid down the 27-meter façade of their building on ropes; mailmen washed cars, and police played badminton continuously for 24 hours. An Adopt-an-Athlete scheme raised over half a million pounds to feed, accommodate and trans-port competitors. And a call for 2,000 volunteers got an overwhelming response. "There were teenagers, mums, dads and grannies," said games director Gordon McCormack, a cheerful Scotsman and former sports organizer for the disabled. "Now we have an army of Glaswegians dedicated to helping people with disabilities."

The local people's generosity and friendliness delight-ed the athletes, some of whom, like Italian champion Palese, had difficulties with their families and were institutionalized. When Adriano was four his mother entrusted him to a local shepherd. Ten years had passed before the authorities were informed. They found Adriano unschooled, introverted and barely able to communicate.

At 18 years old (born November 17, 1972), Adriano moved to a rehabilitation center run by the Trinity Fathers in Venosa in southern Italy, where he's learning to be a mechanic. Running track has changed his life, according to Michele Giorgio, vice-president of Italy's Handicapped Sports Federation: "He went from complete isolation to being constantly surrounded and encouraged." The trip to Glasgow was a further boost, Giorgio added. "Adriano is still shy and withdrawn, but the crowds and applause have greatly affected him."

Scotland's Peter Meechan (born March 12, 1960), was born with a badly cleft palate and mental retardation. "I had ten operations," he recalled, "but I scarcely went out of the house. When I did go to school, the other kids said, 'That Meechan boy is *stupid.*' But my family always protected and supported me."

Running and competing with his brothers, Peter found his outlet in the most grueling of all Special Olympics competitions, the pentathlon — a two-day torture that combines five events: the 100-meter dash, long jump, shot put, high jump and 400-meter run. He earned his gold medal in Glasgow by winning *all five* events in the qualifying round and romping to victory in the final.

> *Running and competing with his brothers, Peter found his outlet in the most grueling of all Special Olympics competitions, the pentathlon — a two-day torture that combines five events . . .*

"Sport gives me a purpose in life," Peter said. He works out four days a week under coach Tom Boyle, whose stable includes two of Britain's top runners: Tom McKean and Yvonne Murray. Peter devotes another day each week to working with other athletes with disabilities, and spends his spare time doing chores for elderly neighbors. "I cut their grass and dig their gardens," he said. "I don't view myself as disabled, and people where I live don't make a fool of me any more. They treat me with respect."

While the games dramatically underscored the importance of giving people with mental retardation

meaningful lives, they also demonstrated the appalling backwardness of Russian and East European societies in this field. "Our society is such that these people are not accepted," sighed Natalia Sladkova, general secretary of the Soviet Federation for Sport for the Disabled. "People see someone with a disability and think, 'What did this man do wrong?' It is difficult for us to change attitudes quickly, but we believe that sports can help bring these barriers down."

Added Hungary's team leader, Miki Hanori, "Most of our citizens with mental retardation are in institutions. They were totally invisible when the Communists were in power." Then he brightened. "But now it is changing. We even had a team from Hungarian national television with us."

One quality that never fails to impress observers of people with disabilities is the depth of their response to kindness. "These people are so appreciative of any attention," said Maria Victoria Graell, coach of the Spanish basketball team. "An encouragement is all they need to animate them."

Certainly, the happiest athletes in Glasgow were those whose families and friends came along to support them. Ireland's Caroline Russell, then 15, brought family and friends from County Donegal to cheer her to a silver medal in an equestrian event for novices. Edgar Poelchau, a stern-faced German army colonel, broke down and cried when his blond, 28-year-old son, Gert, won a gold medal in swimming. "He was typical until he was two," sighed Poelchau. "Then he had a standard childhood injection for measles or whooping cough. Although it almost never happens, the inoculation damaged his brain. He still can't read or write, but now sport is his life."

Everyone's a winner, blazed a headline in Glasgow's *Daily Record,* and it was true. In Special Olympics parlance, athletes who finished eighth, for example, were eighth-place "winners," and awarded ribbons to

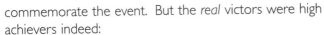

commemorate the event. But the *real* victors were high achievers indeed:

■ Portuguese swimmer Pedro Henriques, 17, took a gold medal in the 4x25 relay and a bronze in the 25-meter freestyle. Just two days earlier he had dived into a pool in Marinha Grande, Portugal, to save a teenager from drowning.

■ Belgian gymnast Alain Strouven, 20, who won bronze medals in the horizontal bar and floor exercises on his first day of competition, called home with the good news. After winning two *golds* the next day in the vault and parallel bars, he said with a grin, "I guess I'll have to make another phone call."

■ Michelle Orlando, 24, a raven-haired pixie from southern France, swept through the round-robin table-tennis tournament, losing a single game to Greece's Maria Prokopa, who was given to skipping with delight whenever she scored a point. In the final, Michelle overcame Maria 21–10 and danced her own jig of joy.

There was much spontaneous hugging in Glasgow. When France's five-man soccer team, whose oldest player was 15, lost to an older Scottish squad on a last-second goal, the French goalkeeper flung himself to the floor in frustration. His whole team, as well as the Scottish and Portuguese teams, piled on to console him. Monaco gymnast Christophe Ierano, at age eight the baby of the Special Olympics, stole the show at the awards ceremony when he had to be pried from the arms of two teenage admirers to accept his silver medal for tumbling. And winners and losers alike lined up to be kissed by Poland's pretty table-tennis coach.

Like Gert, England's Maria Amos, 28, was born without disability, but meningitis at age 18 months damaged her brain. Her parents kept her at home until she was ten, when she was molested by a stranger on her way to school. Maria then spent six years in an institution, where she learned to swim. Back home, she began competing in Special Olympics meets, winning medals in swimming, gymnastics and track. "As she got older, we introduced her to new sports," explained Keith Etches, who runs the Merseyside education center where Maria trains.

"Ooooh, I can't stand it any more," fidgeted her mother as she watched Maria's tense semifinal match in carpet bowls. The indoor equivalent of lawn bowling, carpet bowls is an intricate sport that demands intense concentration, tactical thinking and pinpoint accuracy. New to the game, Maria came nail-bitingly close to victory before losing an overtime bowl-off. Punching the air, she promised, "I'll be back, and next time I'll win."

The magic finally ended. At the jubilant closing ceremony, newfound friends exchanged embraces and addresses. They danced a delirious conga, medals jingling on their proud chests. "We love you, Glasgow!" a French girl shouted, flinging her cap high into the air. Hundreds of other caps instantly followed, to cries of "We love you! We love you!" Glasgow loved them too — every last one.

RYAN'S GREATEST TEST

by William Nack

For years he had played the critical moment over and over in his mind. Now he was about to live it.

MONONGAHELA, PA., lies about 25 miles south of Pittsburgh on the west bank of the river for which it is named. Ryan Bucchianeri grew up there, spending much of his youth at the home of his grandfather, Peno Bucchianeri, on Park Avenue, surely one of the most extraordinary streets in small-town America.

Located on Park as well was the home of Ryan's great-uncle, Mike Bucchianeri, who played for the Green Bay Packers. And young Joe Montana, of Super Bowl fame, only had to step out his door at 512 Park and cross the street to a grassy field to practice throwing footballs. The town was also home to Myron Pottios, the old Pittsburgh Steeler linebacker, and Fred Cox, who kicked for the Minnesota Vikings.

What else was a boy raised in such a neighborhood to do but play football? Says Ryan's mother, Rosemary, "Ryan didn't have much choice. It was predestined."

When Ryan was a young boy, a cousin of his father's, Armand Niccolai, who kicked and played tackle for the Steelers, was already giving him instructions in the family's back yard. He would turn a Styrofoam cup upside down, like a tee, and hold the ball on it for Ryan to kick.

By the time he got to Ringgold High School, Ryan was well along in his quest for the perfect, unflawed kick. District athletic director Paul Zolak could set his watch by the boy. "I'd be driving down the hill, and there'd be Ryan, kicking by himself," says Zolak. "He did it every day. Every day."

"There's a beauty in kicking," Ryan said. But he approached it as a science. Ask him how a five-foot, nine-inch, 150-pound boy could launch a football 60 yards, and he'd answer, "Force equals mass times acceleration. The force I put into the ball is equal to the mass of my leg times how fast I whip it into the ball." He burst at least ten old footballs a year in high school, pounding them toward a distant tree in his yard or drilling them through the goal posts at school.

But there were also other sides to him. On Saturday nights when his parents and younger brother were away, Ryan would turn off the living-room lights and improvise for hours at the piano—now making the keys sound like wind chimes, now making them sound like rain. "I play best in the dark," he'd say. "Everything comes from the heart."

Ryan's grades were nearly perfect. He was a member of the National Honor Society and president of his junior and senior classes. He didn't drink, smoke or swear. He was the most accurate kicker in the history of Ringgold High—he kicked 105 of 108 extra points, as well as a 50-yard field goal—and he was among the nation's most ballyhooed kicking prospects. By the end of his senior year, he was all-state and All-American, a throwback to some Jurassic age of scholar-athlete.

Somewhere along the line, Ryan decided he wanted to be an astronaut and walk on the moon one day. He figured that the U.S. Naval Academy at Annapolis, Md., would be the pathway to his dream. Scores of colleges recruited him, but none had a prayer. He wanted Navy. "The Navy didn't recruit him," says his mother. "He recruited them."

Ryan arrived at the academy on June 30, 1993. Practically the first thing he did was to ask his dad to pull over next to the football practice fields. Ryan dug into the trunk and pulled out his right kicking shoe, its cleats caked with mud from the Ringgold High field. He said, "I want a little bit of something from where I grew up down here with me." So he walked onto the practice field while picking the dirt off the cleats, scattering it about like magic seed.

The academy, from its long-held traditions to its smart salutes, suited the new plebe. Bucchianeri loved falling out in the morning in the shadow of Bancroft Hall — the enormous dorm they call "Mother B." He loved the sound of voices shouting, "Go Navy! Beat Army!" He loved the snap of the day. "You study till 11 P.M. and then you hit that bed and reflect on what you've done that day."

Six games into the season, Chaump threw Bucchianeri in for the first time. He booted the ball clean.

He anguished when he had problems in football. During plebe summer, he had dropped to 135 pounds. "We were saying, 'Gosh, this is a high school All-American?'" says Navy coach George Chaump. "He couldn't kick the ball high — he was hitting linemen in the butt. One day, he apologized to me and I said, 'Don't worry. We'll stay with you. Eat a lot of spaghetti.'"

Six games into the season, Chaump threw Bucchianeri in for the first time. He booted the ball clean. That night, as he returned to Mother B, two sophomores in his company, Autumn Pevzner and Robin Pegram, clapped in admiration as he approached. "Way to go, Mr. Bucchianeri," said Pegram.

"No big deal," Ryan said, pleased.

Soon he faced a bigger deal — Navy's game with Notre Dame. In the first quarter, Chaump called on

Ryan for a 38-yard field goal. He hit it perfectly. Then all of a sudden, Ryan said, "I heard bah-BOOM—the Navy cannon going off—and saw a plume of blue smoke." When he turned around, the Midshipmen were cheering him wildly.

But on December 4, 1993, Ryan Bucchianeri, at age 18, only six months out of high school, was to be truly tested for the first time. It was Navy's annual battle against the Midshipmen's arch rival, the Army cadets of West Point, N.Y., at Giants Stadium in New Jersey.

Army was leading 16–14, but the Midshipmen had driven the ball down to around the Cadets' one-yard line, with six seconds left to play. A three-point field goal, kicked clean between the goal posts, would win it for Navy.

"Booch!" called Coach Chaump, using Bucchianeri's nickname. The young kicker quickly materialized at the coach's shoulder, his eyes blinking under the hollow of a helmet that appeared a size too large.

The coach grabbed him tightly by the arm. "Get in there!"

In all the years Ryan Bucchianeri had played and replayed this moment in his mind—from his Pennsylvania boyhood to his first months at the U.S. Naval Academy—he had always made the kick, the one he had to nail to beat Army. Not once, in all his youthful reveries, had he ever missed.

> *In all the years Ryan Bucchianeri had played and replayed this moment . . . Not once, in all his youthful reveries, had he ever missed.*

Never imagined anything but the kick that sailed, end over end, through the uprights. The boot that lifted the Midshipmen over the Cadets and raised the boy onto the shoulders of his teammates.

All along the Navy bench, Midshipmen stared solemnly. Bucchianeri headed onto the field, repeating the first commandment of place kicking, of which his father had reminded him only the night before: "Keep your head down and follow through."

"Come on, Ryan!" hollered Leon "Red" Romo, the team trainer. "Put it in there and I'll give you an extra steak next week!"

The ball was on the right side of the field, the most difficult angle for a right-legged kicker. And it had been raining, making the task even harder. Adjusting for the angle, Booch bent forward. Then he stepped forward, locked his knee, and swung his leg as if it were a golf club. As he drove his toe into the ball, he thought: *Something's different.*

The kick floated to the right — missing the goal posts by about 18 inches. The referee waved his arms: "No good!"

Ryan turned his back to the goal posts and fell to one knee. Dropping his head, he closed his eyes and raised a hand to his face mask. "I can't believe it," he muttered. "This isn't happening."

In the locker room, Ryan appeared white as a ghost. His teammates thought he was in shock. Then someone told him that the "gentlemen of the press" were waiting.

"Should I go?" he asked.

"If you don't feel like going, don't," said co-captain Jason Van Matre.

Bucchianeri thought a moment. *Be responsible for your actions,* he told himself. Then he turned and left to face the microphones.

First, asked how he felt, he paused, blinking in the camera lights. "I did the best I could," he finally said.

When a reporter gently lobbed him an excuse — wondering about the rain, about the snap of the ball, Bucchianeri let it sail by. "It doesn't matter," he said quietly. "I missed the kick, sir."

It was the hour of his keenest disappointment. But in an age of sport in which losers are lepers — a time when talk is trash and the buck is passed — the kid who missed the kick blamed only himself.

When Ryan arrived back at the Academy he was to hear worse news: three members of his approximately 120-member company, Autumn Pevzner, Robin Pegram and Lisa Winslow, all friends of his, had been killed in a car crash on the way home to Annapolis from New Jersey. No one had felt worse for him when he missed the kick than had those three. Lisa had told her mother in a telephone conversation after the game that she wanted to talk to Ryan to make sure he understood the loss was not his fault, that if the team had done better the game would not have hinged on his kick. "I really want to be there for him when he gets back," she had said.

However, Ryan's sadness over the game was now nothing compared with his anguish over the loss of friends. Football's a game; death is real, he thought. Ryan had finally arrived at a place where he had never been, a place darkened by death and failure and grief.

In the days following the Army–Navy game, he received hundreds of letters offering solace. They came from all places and all kinds of people. One was simply addressed "To the Young Man at the Naval Academy whose place kick missed going through the goal by inches."

The letters were often long and always generous. They spoke of suffering and handling adversity. "People shared some very personal things with me — from striking out in the last inning of a baseball game to captains and admirals losing men in war," Bucchianeri says. "A lot of people said I taught them a lesson — that we can fail sometimes and it's okay as long as you've tried your best."

Bucchianeri was left, of course, to write his own ending to events.

"When times get tough, I'll be able to think to myself: I've been here before," he says. "I can get through it. Some people have it a lot worse."

He went to the Academy's auditorium, turned off the lights and sat down at the piano in the dark. "I was thinking about everything," he says. "How fragile life is at times."

Then, Ryan Joseph Bucchianeri — place kicker and pianist from Monongahela, Pa., began to play — now making the keys sound like wind chimes, now making them sound like rain.

THE ABIDING VISION OF CRAIG MACFARLANE

by Andrew Jones

**This world-class athlete captured 103
gold medals despite his visual impairment.
But then came a much greater challenge.**

STRANGERS were jammed elbow-to-elbow along the Jefferson Memorial concourse in Washington, D.C., on that chill May evening in 1984. The Olympic torch was coming, on its way from New York to Los Angeles.

Suddenly a cheer went up as a pinprick of flame appeared. Then the cheering took on tones of astonishment — for there were *two* athletes in Olympic Relay singlets running side by side. Many recognized the older. "Gordie Howe!" they shouted. The legendary hockey star, smiling left and right, had his hand on the elbow of a handsome young man holding high the flickering brand. "Daddy," a little girl perched on her father's shoulders exclaimed, "he's blind!"

The cheering escalated to a roar as Craig MacFarlane sprinted along in the total darkness he had known since he was only 2½ years old. His face alight with joy, he shouted back to the encouraging voices. *I'm told I'm the greatest athlete who is blind in the world,* he thought. *But what are gold medals compared with this?*

A kilometer down the concourse Craig passed the torch to the next relay runner, and reporters crowded around calling questions:

"Why did you slow down at the end?"

"This is my first run since I tore a hamstring doing a front flip off a water-ski jump."

"What?"

> "If I can 'see' it," he says, "I can do it. Blindness is not a handicap — it's a minor inconvenience."

To Craig MacFarlane there is nothing surprising about his skiing on snow or water or his sinking a 50-foot putt. On a golf green he walks from ball to cup and back, feeling the terrain under his feet, mentally computing its rise or fall.

He calls it "muscle memory." On a ski slope, where he has sped at nearly 60 MPH, he follows the swish of the guide's skis ahead of him. He makes his other senses do the work of vision. "If I can 'see' it," he says, "I can do it. Blindness is not a handicap — it's a minor inconvenience."

The only thing Craig remembers seeing with his eyes was a porcupine in the woods behind the family's farm near Sault Ste. Marie, Ontario. His next memory is of four or five neighborhood children romping outside the toolshed, one of them swinging the striker of a welding torch. Then came a flash of agony as the tool struck Craig in the face. He remembers running, screaming, onto the porch and colliding with the kitchen door. The striker had torn open his left eyeball. Six weeks later, sympathetic ophthalmia took the sight of his right eye.

His memories after that are of his parents and his older brother, Ian, gently urging him to walk forward, follow the sound, use his hands, feel his way around the house and yard. His mother, a teacher, had him run his hands over blueberry bushes to learn how to leave the hard, unripe berries and pick the large, soft ones. These were his first lessons in muscle memory. Soon he could go trapping with his father, milk cows and pitch hay.

Young Craig did a lot of banging into things, stumbling over the wheelbarrow, skinning his shins on the vacuum cleaner, and there were moments when, racked with anger and frustration, he was ready to give up. But the growing boy refused to use a cane or a guide dog and gradually began to develop a sense for the objects in his vicinity. When he talked of becoming a great hockey player, the MacFarlanes did not try to dissuade him. The word "can't" was not spoken in his presence. Craig's family was waiting for him to realize on his own that he would never play team sports.

"There's that blind kid!" When Craig was six his dad drove him 500 miles to the W. Ross MacDonald School for the blind, in Brantford. But he hated it — this place was for blind people! His struggle all along had been to be the equal of sighted boys.

After two years at the school, Craig found a release from his bitterness in sports — he chose wrestling first because body contact, *feel,* was maintained throughout a match. Quick, strong, with lightning reflexes, he twisted beneath his opponent on a takedown and had him in a lock before anyone knew what had happened. He once heard his coach say, "Craig's technique is good, but it's his ability to think quickly that makes the difference."

Still, he felt little joy in the competition. Although he won 20 matches in a row, each time he was led into a gym he would hear the whispers: "There's that blind kid!" *I have a name,* he would think bitterly. *And before this day is over, you guys will know what it is!*

Craig entered swim meets, went for the gold, and more often than not he took it. On the cinder track he ran all the sprint distances. His coaches taught him to heft the javelin and discus and watched in wonder as he unwound his body with a seemingly effortless rhythmic power.

These sports, Craig found, were less intense than wrestling and more fun — the prodigious will to win was still there, but without the blood-fury of pinning the other man's shoulders to the canvas. And now he was making friends and broadening his horizons. He took lessons on the clarinet, piano and trumpet. He was beginning to think the life of darkness ahead of him had a lot of potential. Perhaps he would study politics and law.

Growing Reputation. For now, however, Craig decided that his immediate future lay in sports, and that he would aim for the top. During his high-school years he approached the peak of his athletic ability, working his way to a future grand total of 11 national and 6 international championships in wrestling, skiing, swimming, discus, javelin and track.

In his first year at Carleton University in Ottawa, on the strength of his growing reputation, he talked Molson Breweries into sponsoring the "Craig MacFarlane Molson Celebrity Tennis Classic," a tournament to raise money for research on blindness in Canada. Gordie Howe, originally from Saskatchewan, served as honorary chairman.

Gordie and Colleen Howe took instantly to Craig, this 19-year-old who had put the tournament together. Craig told them his mother was American and that one of his ambitions was to visit the land of her birth. The Howes invited Craig to spend a week at their summer cottage in Michigan and, not long after, Craig decided to move to the United States. The Howes were delighted. At their insistence, Craig moved into their home in Connecticut.

Gordie, now special assistant to the chairman of the Hartford Whalers hockey team, hired the young athlete as a ticket salesman. Craig kept to his training regimen before and after work, entering competitions on weekends.

Invited to serve as spokesman at the first national water-skiing championships for the sight impaired at Florida's Cypress Gardens, Craig accepted on condition that he be allowed to compete. The event consisted of swerving back and forth across the towboat wake, the winner determined by the number of crossings in a given time. Craig practiced a few hours and won the trophy,

then mentioned that he would like to go off the ski jump. It had never been attempted by a sightless skier. "When?" the officials asked. "Right now," he replied.

A professional skied at his elbow, shouting, "Four . . . three . . . two . . . one." But the towrope was torn from Craig's hands on the first try as he crashed into the water. He insisted on another attempt — and then made nine perfect takeoffs and landings in a row.

Blank Wall. In the spring of 1984 Craig was asked to join athletes campaigning for the re-election of President Reagan. At the big kick-off, flanked by Joe Frazier and Floyd Patterson on the steps of the Philadelphia Museum of Art, he spoke of the President's efforts on behalf of people with physical disabilities. The roaring ovation from the crowd established him as a campaign star.

He left the campaign in August to enter the sixth annual International Ridder Games, the world-water-skiing championships for the visually impaired held in Norway. Out of shape, with no time to train, he placed fourth. This defeat was a real comeuppance — Craig MacFarlane rarely came in fourth at anything. Was he finished as an athlete?

. . . he looked at his future, and discovered he was staring at a blank wall.

Craig returned to the Reagan-Bush re-election campaign, and by November had addressed 231 audiences in 39 states. On the first night of the Republican National Convention in Dallas, Craig stepped up before 13,000 people to speak into the auditorium's glare and thunder.

To the 22-year-old former farm boy, rubbing elbows with national candidates and some of the greatest names in American sports had been heady stuff. But now he looked at his future, and discovered he was staring at a blank wall.

It was not in Craig's nature to give in to the depression that started to plague him. He began to think again about the sweat, the preparation, the training, physical and mental, that he had packed into his life so far. He had to believe that it added up to something. *I must trust myself,* he concluded.

Jobless, with his ever-encouraging parents supporting him, Craig moved in with friends in Houston and began reviewing his options. The year before he had taken some time off and, sitting alone on a beach in Maine, had tape-recorded a list of his accomplishments. Reviewing them, he realized that he was still fighting his "minor inconvenience," desperate to have his name known to everyone as it had been in his early wrestling days.

He also saw how foolish he had been to think he could ever make his way on his own. His life had been full of people who had been there when he needed them. Craig now understood he had accomplished nothing for which he did not have to share credit with a supporting cast that rose in his memory by the dozens. It was, he realized, time to learn a little humility — and to do some giving of his own.

In early 1985, Craig became a consultant to the President's Council on Physical Fitness and Sports to speak with and inspire young people with disabilities. At the same time, a chain of fitness centers hired him to deliver motivational speeches to employees around the country.

But although the 102 gold medals in his trunk were becoming less important to his self-image, he still wanted one more — the one he had flubbed in Norway the year before. After weeks of intensive physical training, he flew there again in pursuit of it. And on August 9, 1985, Craig MacFarlane set a new world record — 34 wake crossings in 40 seconds.

The Torch Is Passed. Back in Texas two weeks later, Craig was standing up to his waist in a lake and demonstrating special swimming techniques to a group of Boy Scouts with visual impairments. He was concentrating on a 14-year-old whose overprotective parents had never let him near a large body of water. As Craig strapped a life jacket on the boy, he thought of his own parents and the encouragement and freedom they had given him. "Come on, Champ!" he urged. "I'm right here with you. I'm blind. I can do it — and so can you!"

In a few minutes Craig had the boy jumping off the dock into his arms. *This,* he thought, *is a hundred times better than traveling and talking!* Next they climbed into a water-skiing towboat. The boy was terrified, but Craig kept holding his hand up to feel the wind and down to feel the water rushing past.

Finally they both put on skis and, with Craig's arms around his waist, the boy had the thrill of skimming along the lake's surface. "In another couple of years," Craig told the boy, "you'll be beating the pants off me. Then I'll *have* to retire!"

And that, he thought suddenly, *is the way it's supposed to be.*

Football Hall-of-Famer Andy Robustelli, Craig's confidant and personal adviser, talks about this moment: "It was a new kind of victory. It was another way to *win.* In sports you're always trying to beat the other fellow. This time Craig was trying to help somebody . . . and he *still* won."

Craig talks about it too: "I told the boy I was blind. I said it out loud, and for the first time in my life I really believed it. It was like passing the torch that afternoon in Washington; I was passing it to him. He and I were on the same side. I was a team player after all."

PRIDE OF
THE NAVAJOS

by Suzanne Chazin

**Through example, one man and a
group of teenagers taught their
community how to reach for the stars**

ACONSTANT ROAR thunders inside
Albuquerque's Tingley Coliseum where two
girls' basketball teams are about to play for
New Mexico's 1988 high-school championship. Coach
Jerry Richardson peers at the stands. He sees old
women in colorful dresses and turquoise jewelry raise
their arms to form a wave. He hears ecstatic Navajo
children calling out players' names.

They are cheering for the Lady Chieftains from
Shiprock, a desert town on the Navajo Nation reservation. They are cheering for a group of high-school girls
who have known few victories in life, led by a black
coach who will not accept defeat. In eight years of living
with these normally reserved people, Richardson has
never seen them so aroused.

Dressed in simple maroon-and-gray uniforms, the mostly short, stocky teen-agers look tense. They are up against Kirtland-Central High School's powerhouse Lady Broncos, who have won eight state championships in a row.

In the pregame huddle, coach Richardson reminds his team, "We can win this." He speaks in a calm, serious voice that gives no hint of his Texarkana, Texas, upbringing. "I believe in you. Now *you* have to believe." The girls emerge from the huddle shouting their coach's favorite exhortation, "Discipline!"

As Richardson watches the Lady Chieftains take the court, he senses the nervous hope they share with their fans. This is a chance to prove that the Navajo people can achieve anything they set their hearts on.

> *At Shiprock High School, teachers came and left as frequently as spring snows on the mesa.*

In 1980, Jerry Richardson was hired as a special-education teacher for Shiprock High School. Then 24, he had just gotten his master's degree in physical education from Louisiana Tech. Before that, he had gone to Northwestern State University of Louisiana on a track scholarship.

Visiting Shiprock for the first time, Richardson felt as if he were in a Third World country: three stoplights, a few broken-down trailers, a couple of convenience stores. Flat, scrubby land stretched for miles, broken only by a large rock shaped like a ship under sail, for which the town is named.

Poverty and unemployment claimed almost one of every two on the reservation. Alcohol and drug abuse were major health problems. Many young people in Shiprock had lost close friends or family to alcohol-related fatalities. Richardson heard rumors of what passed for fun in this bleak area: a game of "chicken." Young people would get drunk and dodge traffic, sometimes with fatal results.

At Shiprock High School, teachers came and left as frequently as spring snows on the mesa. On any day, at least 15 percent of students were absent. And the dropout rate was twice the state average.

When Richardson became the assistant basketball coach, the Lady Chieftains had never won a championship. And no one had expected them to. He had visions of what the team could be, but he didn't get off to the kind of start he wanted. As he was driving to a school game, a truck crossed the median and collided head-on with his car. Richardson was pinned inside for two hours with a punctured lung, a broken jaw and multiple bone fractures.

Four months after the accident, he was back on the basketball court. If Jerry Richardson could pull through a near-fatal car accident without giving up or making excuses, couldn't he foster that same kind of grit in the Lady Chieftains?

Three years later, when the head coach quit, Richardson was the only one interested in the job. He immediately made changes. The girls and their parents were given contracts to sign. Practices would be three hours a day. Three unexcused absences would get a girl kicked off the team.

Instead of waiting for a failed report card to take action, he started weekly grade checks. The players had to act like role models on court and off — no drinking, drugs or discourteous behavior. Dating was fine, but serious boyfriends were out.

One thing that bothered Richardson was the girls' seeming passivity. When he spoke to them, they avoided eye contact. "To them, looking an adult in the eye is rude," another teacher explained. "You can't go against their culture."

"That's fine at home," the coach answered. "But what about off the reservation? People will assume they're submissive or deceitful." So Richardson began to teach the girls to look people in the eye away from home.

He was also annoyed by the informal coaching of relatives. Navajo culture places a strong emphasis on family. Outside of coaching, that was fine with Richardson. But he resented relatives giving advice from the sidelines during a game. "I am their only coach," he told players' families.

Richardson was unprepared for the backlash that followed. Parents complained that he was too strict and not sensitive enough to Navajo culture. Some parents wouldn't speak to him.

"I respect your culture," Richardson would reply. "But I will not handicap these girls. And I will not expect less of them than I expect of myself."

Once, just before a game, Richardson entered the locker room to find 12 adults around a table where one of his players was lying.

"She's witched," an adult explained, pointing to the teenager. "That's why she's not playing well. We have to unwitch her."

Richardson called the team out on the floor. "I want all the girls who believe they're witched to stand to one side," he said. "The rest of us are going to play basket-ball." Suddenly, the girl who was lying on the table no longer believed she was witched.

When parents complained that Richardson had no respect for their religious beliefs, he stood his ground. "I have been teaching these girls that they cannot make excuses. They've got to have the confidence to see tough things through," he said. No girl ever mentioned being "witched" again.

To bolster his program, the coach started summer basketball clinics to train youngsters. Some girls on his early teams had never been off the reservation. He began to take the team on the road for games, checking the girls into first-class motels. He took some of his best players to camps in North Carolina and Pennsylvania where he worked in summers.

"Many Shiprock girls left school and stayed on the reservation," says Richardson. "How does a girl know if that's what she wants to do if she hasn't done anything else? I wanted to show them what opportunities are out there."

Everyone knew coach Richardson was tough, but no one knew how tough until the 1984–85 season. The team's most talented player came to practice two weeks late. She assumed she was so good that the coach wouldn't kick her off the team. She was wrong. "If you are going to be a Lady Chieftain, do it right. If not, forget it," he told her and then dismissed her.

At one point, so many left the team that he was down to 15 girls — including junior-varsity players. But he didn't ease up. "You're being too hard on us," one teenager complained. "Who cares about basketball, anyway?"

"I'm not here just to teach you basketball," the coach replied. "What you learn on this court will carry you through life."

At Tingley Coliseum, it's half time now, and the Lady Chieftains trail 37–28. The girls have played intelligently, passing the ball when pressed, grabbing rebounds. But they can't seem to keep the Broncos from scoring — the same position they were in last year. In the state championship for the first time, they had lost to Kirtland 62–61 in double overtime.

Richardson watches Vernetta Begay hustle off the court. Shoulders hunched, the petite forward appears ready to cry. She has sunk six baskets so far, but her team is still behind. She catches her coach's eye and straightens up. Hasn't he taught her never to quit?

Richardson knew all about wanting to quit things, he said. . . . "No matter what you have in life . . . you can make it better if you see things through."

A year earlier, Vernetta had been devastated by the death of her beloved grandfather. She started hanging around with a fast crowd. She told the coach she wanted to quit basketball.

"Look me in the eye and tell me you want to quit," Richardson ordered. Vernetta couldn't do it. "You've been listening to other people telling you to quit," he told Vernetta. "People who can't succeed themselves just want to pull you down."

Richardson knew all about wanting to quit things, he said. When he was 13, he'd attended a newly integrated junior high. There, he became a receiver on the football team, but the white quarterback never threw him the ball, even in practice.

When he complained to his mother, a nurse's aide, she told him, "It's not the school's fault. It's not the coach's fault. You chose to be there. You made a commitment. Now see it through." He stayed with football, and the following year went out for basketball, determined to be so good that no one could keep him down again.

"No matter what you have in life," he told Vernetta, "you can make it better if you see things through." Vernetta stayed with the team, made new friends and began improving her grades.

> "We have to work harder than we have ever worked before. It's your game, but you've got to take it."

With renewed confidence, the Lady Chieftains fight back in the second half. They're two points down with 15 seconds remaining when Vernetta hits a shot that ties the game at 58, setting up a three-minute overtime.

Richardson tells the girls, "We have to work harder than we have ever worked before. It's your game, but you've got to take it."

Sherri Henderson feels as if the coach is talking just to her. Her parents had split up soon after her birth, and times were often tough. She loved basketball. But then knee surgery side-lined her in her sophomore year, and she fell in with young people who drank.

Richardson told her that she had two choices in life. She could either continue the way she was going and blame her problems on others, or she could take responsibility for herself. "Successful people don't blame others," he told her.

One minute and 37 seconds into overtime, Sherri Henderson takes possession of the ball, 17 feet from the Broncos' basket. It looms up over a flurry of hands trying to block her. Coach Richardson has taught her to look to the goal and rely on her courage and determination to reach it.

Sherri takes aim and shoots. A momentary hush falls as fans follow the ball's long arc. Then, in a sudden swoosh, the hard rubber meets the nylon net. The shot is good!

When the buzzer sounds, the Lady Chieftains have beaten the Broncos 60–58. Cheers ring out as the girls tearfully hug one another, then surround their coach in an embrace. They are winners.

These days when Jerry Richardson drives from his home to Shiprock High School, he passes the town's adolescent drug and alcohol treatment center, opened in 1989, and a dirt field where a community center is planned. The high school itself is the site of the town's new indoor pool.

At school, he sometimes sees former players. Vernetta Begay will stop by to shoot baskets with new players and talk to Richardson. Currently a junior attending Northwest Oklahoma State University on a basketball scholarship, she is planning to return to Shiprock to help Richardson coach full-time after she earns her master's degree.

Shiprock High School's trophy case now boasts three girls' state basketball championship trophies, 1988, '89 and '90. Of the dozens of girls who have gone through Richardson's program, almost all finished high school. More than half are living outside Shiprock, and many have gone on to higher education.

For a group of Navajo teenagers who thought Shiprock was the end of the earth, Jerry Richardson provided the inspiration to reach for the stars.

UNDER THE SPELL OF THE TOUR DE FRANCE

by Daniel Gouverneur

**His bicycle career over, Daniel Gouverneur —
like thousands of others — couldn't stay
away from the greatest race of them all.**

EVERY JULY new pages are written to enrich the
legend of the Tour de France — the world's most
important and exciting bicycle race. For three
weeks France will vibrate to the rhythm of the pack and
cheer the leader in his yellow jersey — and once more
bestow a tremendous ovation on the first man to burst
onto Paris's Avenue des Champs-Élysées. The "Big Loop"
will have worked its magic again.

As a former bicycle racer, Daniel Gouverneur has
endured the hellish mountain laps and has known the
intoxication of the winner's circle. But his lifelong
enthusiasm for racing has never waned. Now a motorcycle monitor of the Tour, he takes us behind the scenes
to share the thrill and excitement — the courage and
heartbreak — of this great sporting event.

Elbow to elbow, neck and neck, French champion Bernard Hinault and young American hero Greg LeMond clawed their way over the final two peaks of the day in the famous Briançon–Alpe d'Huez stage of the 1985 Tour de France. It was a magnificent battle, especially when you consider that they were on the same team!

My motorcycle had spun me ahead of the two sweat-soaked warriors, and I looked down on the grueling climb's multiple switchbacks from the summit. "Watch closely, Gouverneur," a journalist advised me, "you're sitting on history's balcony." As it happened, Hinault and LeMond decided to cross the finish line together. And indeed I witnessed one of the greatest moments in the Tour de France.

That was my fifth time on the glorious race. My job? For 11 months of the year, I'm a press motorcyclist. That is, I transport mail, photos, film, even journalists, from production companies to the airport, from the airport to TV stations. For the twelfth month, my summer vacation, I'm a motorcyclist on the Tour de France, transmitting instructions from team captains, race commissioners, journalists and cyclists to and fro along the day's course. I'm the Tour's combination sheep dog and good Samaritan. Sometimes I have to call the race physician to the aid of a rider in distress, or I may have to impose a slowdown on the convoy of team cars. Apart from being useful, my function also satisfies my greatest passion. For between myself and the Tour de France there's been a love affair for 25 years.

How could I ever forget my feelings that day in the homestretch of the 1967 Race of the Future amateur event? We had just wheeled onto the pink track at the Parc des Princes stadium in Paris. I was with the French team headed by Cyrille Guimard. Tightly packed for the sprint, avid to devour the track, we were riding on air, borne along by the roar of the crowd. That moment was one of the most satisfying in my whole life. Then it was over: Christian Robini won the race; Guimard won the lap. My immediate future was laid out: I would remain an amateur only long enough to participate in the Friendship Games about to begin in Africa. For the next

Tour de France, I would ride as a professional.

But my dreams collapsed under an attack of amebic dysentery just before the Games that sapped me for months. I couldn't hope to participate in the 1968 Tour. And I could not regain the level I'd once reached. At age 22, I suddenly had to wipe away all my career hopes.

The spell of the Tour de France, however, isn't that easy to break. In the 1970s I became a press motorcycle outrider, as many ex-racers do. Then, in 1981, Jean-François Pecheux, a friend and a member of the Tour's management board, suggested I go along as "No. 1 Management Motorcycle." I've worked with every Tour since then. And each year, when the teams stretch out like a multicolored snake along the roads of France, the same miracle occurs.

A pack of 200 racers never moves in a straight line, and certainly not in single file. Not even a champion can jockey himself out of the bunch by pumping straight ahead in the middle of the road. Breakaways are always made along the flanks, protected from the wind by the throngs of spectators and zigzagging to prevent other contestants from gaining an advantage. The first man to light out after the fugitive does the same thing. Then the whole pack follows like a huge, striped caterpillar. It's one of the finest sights I know.

> ... the pack takes up the entire road, whether it is straight or twisty — which means constant maneuvering to find and hold a strategic spot.

The racers' trajectory on twisting roads varies with their number. If there are no more than ten, they take curves like Formula 1 auto-racing drivers, cutting across the bends to avoid using their brakes. They have the whole road to themselves, the Tour being the only race for which all other traffic is stopped. But the pack takes up the entire width of the road, whether it is straight or twisty — which means constant maneuvering to find and hold a strategic spot.

Something is always happening in the pack. There are jokers, like France's Gilbert Duclos-Lassalle, the top-

ranking teammate of American Greg LeMond, who enjoys coming up behind rivals and suddenly screaming. Their startled wobbling sets the rest of the pack laughing. There are the nice guys who share their drinking water with their tortured companions; the dandies who carefully comb their hair every five miles; the hypochondriacs who don't like to get too far away from the course physician; and the worriers, for whom the saddle is never quite the right height.

Riding in the pack is living dangerously. Not when a team is working together on a tactical maneuver and everyone is concentrating on avoiding accidents. But when things slow down and torpor invades the racers, when the summer heat on long, flat stretches dulls their sense of caution. That's when you fail to anticipate the slight jog of the man in front of you, the ensuing slowdown, the wheel smacking against yours. Then there's a fall, often hard, sometimes bloody. It can take you out of the race with a fractured finger, collarbone or leg.

The greatest danger lies at the end of a lap, when the riders are charging forward at 35 miles an hour, heads down, noses close to the handlebars, toward a Tour de France racer's worst enemy — a highway traffic island. Only those in front have time to spot it. For the others — and often for us motorcyclists — it's a matter of luck.

An example? The accident on July 10, 1991, a scant 2.5 miles from the finish line of the Rheims–Valenciennes lap. After a 90-mile run, the pack streamed full-speed into a rotary junction — and a pileup. The men picked themselves up and hobbled off, but one was weeping. He was Rolf Sörensen, and he wore the leader's yellow jersey. This was the first time a Dane had ever led in the race. Now his left collarbone was broken and dislocated.

The next day the Tour moved out of Arras with no one wearing the yellow jersey. This has been the tradition since Spain's Luis Ocana fell coming down off the Mente pass in 1971: the racer who inherits the coveted shirt from a man disabled by an accident does not wear it on the first day he acquires it. Last year LeMond respected this unwritten rule.

Tactics count heaviest on mountain laps. A team leader may send his men out in the lead, ordering them to wear out the others before breaking off. Or he might let a couple of his men lead the pack over a peak or two. If he is up to it physically, the leader can then break out of the pack, join his teammates and pick up added speed from the draft of air they create before pulling away from his rivals. Louison Bobet did this in 1953 after being sucked along in Adolphe Deledda's wake to the foot of the Izoard Pass.

While all riders who make the Tour are world class, not all are strong on hills. Those who are not will never reach the finish line unless they organize their own mini-competition over the Iseran and the Ventoux, the Tourmalet and the Chartreuse — some of the Tour's more infamous climbs. They bunch up far behind the leaders in what is called "the bus." By pedaling at a steady pace, they can rest and still stay within the lap time. In "the bus" you share everything — sweat and water bottles, suffering and pain, courage and heartbreak. You are all in it to survive and to keep the banner of hope flying.

No other sport is as demanding as cycling. A competitor may absorb and eliminate six to ten liters of liquid on a single lap. For a foot racer a 100-meter dash means ten seconds of intense effort, and a marathon requires 2-plus hours of torment. But the Tour de France is a three-week contest that sometimes involves variations in altitude of 3,500 feet in a single day and temperature spans of up to 50 degrees, that keeps the contestants straining for eight to ten hours a day in rain, frost or torrid heat. All this on one or two meals wolfed down as they pedal, spiced with the problems of eliminating what they've ingested, mixed with an occasional flat tire or mechanical failure and, possibly, peppered with falls. Maybe only madmen can enjoy such competition.

I think of the Tour's legends while I follow the road. "Beloved" Charles Pélissier; "Cannibal" Eddy Merckx; "Master Jacques" Anquetil; Federico Bahamontes, the

You are all in it to survive and to keep the banner of hope flying.

"Eagle of Toledo"; and Bernard Hinault, "the Badger" — were they all mad? Certainly theirs are some of the finest achievements in modern sports.

I know that again this year I, like millions of French, will recall the highlights of the past. For example, the day in 1947 when Jean Robic, a.k.a. "Leatherhead," struggled up the Bonsecours hill outside of Rouen to become the first man to win the Tour without ever having worn the yellow jersey. Or when in 1950 Belgium's Maurice Blomme had to be helped by race officials to cross the finish line in Perpignan after collapsing of heatstroke 50 yards from his goal.

I think of Fausto Coppi, alone in the lead, climbing the formidable Puy de Dôme and the Alpe d'Huez, included in the race for the first time in 1952; of the way Bobet soared over the Izoard in 1953; of the day in 1958 when Raphael Geminiani wept at the top of the Chartreuse pass into the torn yellow jersey he would never wear back to Paris; of Anquetil's victory in his hometown of Rouen and of his fabled duel with Raymond Poulidor on the Puy de Dôme in 1964. Finally, of the day in 1983 when Pascal Simon, although still leading, had to drop out after racing seven laps with a broken collarbone.

Of the men I have followed in my 12 years as a monitor, Hinault impressed me most: He was a born winner. His chances were rated low after a fall in a sprint at Saint-Étienne in 1985 that left him with a bloody head. He was hospitalized that evening, but the next morning he was back in the starting line. Although he was having trouble breathing, he went on to win the '85 Tour.

The devotion given to cycling stars is doubtless based partly on the fact that they struggle more for glory than for fortune. When Jean-Marie Leblanc, now the Tour manager, went professional in 1967, his monthly salary was 500 francs — around $100. Each member of Belgium's Hitachi team won about 4,600 francs at the end of three weeks' racing in 1989. True, the Tour winner that year pocketed 1.5 million francs (around $300,000), and since 1990 first place has paid two million francs. But the prize money distributed to the rest of the field is markedly lower than the take in other sports.

This is mainly because the public has never had to pay to watch the Tour. Yet the spectators clearly understand the human and moral value of effort. Perhaps this is why so many of them line the roads when the procession speeds through.

You have to follow a Tour to get an idea of what the crowd is like. The arrival at l'Alpe d'Huez is a case in point. Emerging from Bourg d'Oisans, the Tour route curves left, then right toward a mountain slope held in check by a huge stone retaining wall. Then it veers left up a 12-degree slope 200 yards long. This is just the first of 22 switchbacks that carry the leaders to the top.

The now legendary six-mile ascent is clogged by 250,000 to 400,000 spectators who will stop at nothing to reach a prime observation post. They form a moving wall that opens reluctantly, momentarily, only to close immediately behind each racer, each car, each motorcycle. To those who have experienced this lap, it's surrealistic: the high pastures turned into fairgrounds, the usually deserted, peaceful mountain transformed into a gigantic anthill, the clamor rising and swelling. You advance into a rising howl that won't die out until much later, when the crowd descends, bumper to bumper, back down into the valley.

Give all this up? I'd rather not think about it. I'll be at the starting line again each year, and the next, for as long as I am asked to be there. I know I will always feel the same emotional swelling in the Alps, the same thrill when the first rider darts onto the Champs-Élysées and is greeted by a million cheering spectators. I also know that each Tour will be different from all those that came before it.

> *The now legendary six-mile ascent is clogged by 250,000 to 400,000 spectators who will stop at nothing to reach a prime observation post.*

The next yearly Tour de France, held in 1992, was won by Miguel Indurain of Spain. The calm 28 year old Indurain beat out second place Claudio Chiappucci of Italy, taking his second consecutive win and setting a new record for the fastest average speed for the Tour (39.504 kph). He became the first Spaniard and the sixth rider ever to win both the Tours of France and Italy in the same season.

THE LOUDEST CHEER

by Michael Bowker

In the history of baseball, few players with his handicap had made it to the Major Leagues. But Curtis Pride had his reasons to keep trying.

SLUMPED on the locker-room bench, the young ballplayer was oblivious to the noise of showers and banging lockers of the other players. Curtis Pride was trying to concentrate his thoughts.

In the past few weeks he had broken up with his girlfriend, and he missed his family back home in Silver Spring, Md. Now, his minor-league team, the Binghamton (N.Y.) Mets, had lost another game. Pride had struck out, extending a batting slump that summer of 1992.

As Pride pulled off his jersey, he felt as low as he could get. Then turning his head suddenly, he caught sight of his teammates. One was gaping stupidly, in mocking fashion. Another held his hand behind his ear as if he were deaf. Others were laughing. When they saw Pride looking, they stopped and turned to their lockers.

Curt fought for breath. *My own teammates!* He stood and faced the taunting players. The locker room grew quiet as Pride, fists clenched, his powerful six-foot frame tensed, walked slowly toward the two men.

Pride stopped just inches away. "I can't hear you, but I can think and I can feel, just like you," he said in carefully measured tones. "My handicap is deafness. Yours is intolerance. I'd rather have mine."

The players were surprised by the eloquent words, so unlike what is usually heard in a locker room. They looked away, embarrassed.

As he turned to leave, Pride suddenly wanted to quit. All his years of effort and sacrifice, seemed to come to nothing. His dream of becoming a Major League baseball player, the first deaf one in nearly 50 years, was fading.

When their robust baby boy Curtis was born in December 1968, Sallie Pride, a registered nurse, and her husband, John, a consulting firm executive, were ecstatic.

By the time Curt was five months old, however, Sallie was worried about her boy's vocal sounds, which were often high-pitched screeches. One morning Sallie and John sat Curt down and knelt behind him. "Curt," Sallie called out softly. The boy didn't respond. Then John called, louder. Curt didn't move. Finally, desperate, John shouted, "Curtis!" There was no response.

Sallie looked at her husband with tears in her eyes. "Our baby can't hear us," she said.

With an irreversible 95-percent hearing loss, Curt attended special classes in his Washington, D.C., suburb. Sallie and John chose a program to help their son read lips, aware that some children who used sign language never learned to speak because they could fall back on the signing when they were misunderstood.

"He feels isolated enough already," John told Sallie. "I think sports might help. He can meet other kids and compete on an equal footing." They enrolled six-year-old Curt in a local Tee-ball league, a youth baseball program.

Curt came to the plate in his first game with a runner on base. Sallie and John watched from the stands as he hit the ball over the center fielder's head. Curt flew around first and caught up with the other runner before they reached second. Unsure of the rules, Curt hesitated, then darted around the slower boy.

Laughing, Sallie and John shouted, "No! No!" But Curt, his eyes alive with excitement, tore around third and raced home. "I'm going to be a baseball player!" he repeated over and over that night.

In fourth grade, Curt took some regular classes with hearing students. "I'm finally going to be with all the other kids," he told his mother excitedly. But the first day, Curt came home vowing never to return. Boys had mocked his different speech throughout the day.

Sallie wrapped Curt in her arms. "There will always be cruel people," she said. "But you can never, ever let them stop you from doing what you want to do."

From that day forward, Curt wore his mother's advice like armor.

In seventh grade, Curt was given the choice of continuing his special classes or attending a nearby junior high. Against the advice of school authorities, Curt chose the neighborhood school. "I know I can do it," he pleaded. His parents agreed.

Curt's teachers tried to remember that he depended on lip-reading, but on occasion they forgot and spoke facing the blackboard. Outside class, Curt struggled futilely to follow the other students' conversations.

By the end of the first week, he knew he needed help. He talked it out with his father. "Sometimes," John told him, "you have to be brave enough to trust someone."

The following Monday, when a shy student named Steve Grupe sat down beside him, Curt took that chance. "Hi, I'm Curt Pride, and I'm having a little trouble," he said. "I wonder if you can help."

To his relief, the boy smiled. "Sure," he said, "if you'll give me some baseball pointers!"

The boys became inseparable, studying at each other's houses and playing soccer and baseball in the park.

> *In seventh grade, Curt was given the choice of continuing his special class or attending a nearby junior high. Against the advice of school authorities, Curt chose the neighborhood school.*

Steve helped Curt take notes, and when teachers turned their backs in class, he mouthed their words. As Curt, excelling in sports, became popular in school, he introduced Steve to everyone he met.

In high school Curt won national recognition in soccer and set school records in basketball. But baseball was his first love. After high school, he was drafted by the New York Mets and also accepted a basketball scholarship from the College of William and Mary.

Not until he graduated from college could Pride turn to baseball full time. In 1991 at the Mets' level-A farm club in the Florida State League, he attended spring training and played a full season for the first time. The year proved disappointing. Though Curt was good enough to get promoted to the Binghamton AA team in 1992, he wasn't considered a strong Major League prospect. In Binghamton his play deteriorated. Finally, he was benched. Pride became withdrawn. Then the locker-room taunting occurred, deepening his summer slump.

Feeling despondent, Pride called his parents on his text telephone, a computerlike machine with a keyboard and small screen. "I think the Mets have lost faith in me," he typed. "I'm not sure I want to go on."

That night, John and Sallie drove to Binghamton. The next morning they took Curt to breakfast near the team's hotel. "Honor your commitment to finish the season," his father advised. "Then, if you choose not to play baseball, that's fine. Just make sure it's your decision."

At home after the season ended, Pride thought seriously about giving up on baseball. He began to think that deafness really was too big an obstacle to overcome. Then something changed his mind.

Curt Pride returned to a job he had enjoyed during the previous off-season, helping students with learning and physical disabilities at his old high school. Now he was asked to tutor a class of ninth-graders.

On his first day, Pride sat beside a dark-haired boy. "I don't need your help," the boy snapped. "Stay away."

All the students were watching, and Pride knew he was being tested. "I'm only here to help show you what you can do," he responded, "not tell you what you can't."

Within a week, the students were peppering Pride with questions about baseball and being deaf. Then one day, the dark-haired boy asked Pride, "Aren't you afraid people are laughing behind your back?"

"You just have to be tough enough to ignore them," Pride answered. "What matters isn't what they think, but what you think about yourself."

On his last day, the entire class crowded around. "You're cool, man. We'll be following your career," said one boy.

Pride scanned their faces. How could he admit that his own challenge was too great? "I'd be letting them, and myself, down if I quit now," he later told his mother.

Before baseball season began, Pride got an offer from the Montreal Expos. When the Expos promised he would play every day, he quickly agreed.

At the team's Harrisburg, Pa., farm club, manager Jim Tracy knew Pride's strengths — and his weaknesses. He persuaded Pride to forget home runs and concentrate on getting on base, where he could use his speed.

Pride started the 1993 season brimming with confidence. Hitting to all fields, he tore up the league. In late June, Pride was promoted to the Expos' AAA farm club in Ottawa. By September he was wondering whether he would get a shot at the Majors that season.

On September 11, Pride was outside the locker room when Mike Quade asked to see him. Pride and his teammates often played good-natured jokes on one another, and Pride figured he was being set up.

He walked cautiously into the locker room and saw Quade, smiling, on the telephone. From across the room, he lip-read Quade's final sentence: "Yeah, I'll tell Curt he's being called up."

Pride felt a thrill. He was being called up to the Major Leagues!

Curt Pride was startled when Montreal Expos manager Felipe Alou yelled out his name. The Philadelphia Phillies were leading Montreal 7–4 in the seventh inning. With one out and two runners on base, Pride thought

Alou would send in a more experienced pinch hitter. But Alou was calling him.

In his first time at bat a few days before, Pride had driven the ball deep to right. "I can hit Major League pitching!" he told his parents. Now his old friend Steve Grupe was in the stands to watch him play, and his new team was depending on him.

Bobby Thigpen, the Phillies' flame-throwing relief pitcher, was on the mound. As Pride gripped the bat, Thigpen fired a hard slider. Pride waited; then at the last moment his bat exploded across the plate. The ball shot like a bullet between the outfielders and bounced all the way to the wall.

Racing around first, Pride slid into second in a cloud of dust. Safe! Both runners scored! Steve Grupe leapt up, pummeled the air with his fists and whooped.

Excited, Pride looked to third-base coach Jerry Manuel to see if he could steal on the next pitch. But Manuel was motioning to the stands. Pride looked up. All 45,000 fans were on their feet, stamping and cheering.

As Pride stood, frozen, the thunderous ovation continued. Manuel motioned for Curt to doff his cap.

Then, as the stamping and cheering reached a crescendo, something incredible happened. It started as a vibrating rumble, then grew more intense until, for the first time in his life, Curt Pride actually heard people cheering for him. The curtain of silence had parted.

> **With one out and two runners on base, Pride thought Alou would send in a more experienced pinch hitter. But Alou was calling him.**

Montreal Expo Curtis Pride proved his big-league potential that first season with four hits in nine at bats — a .444 average. In addition to his double, he banged a triple and a home run.

"My message for people with disabilities — or to any person who has been told he can't do something — is simple," says Pride. "Ignore it. The answers are inside your own heart."

SYLVIE FRÉCHETTE: TRIUMPH OVER TRAGEDY

by Jean Gounelle

Despite loss and pain, Canada's heroine of synchronized swimming follows her dream.

S tanding high on the podium at the Montreal Forum, the slender young woman shyly acknowledges the sea of fans, 7,000 of them, who have come to share her moment of glory. Sixteen months after the 1992 Olympic Games in Barcelona, Sylvie Fréchette is finally awarded the gold medal she deserved but was denied because of a judge's error.

Thousands of voices chant her name. You mustn't cry, the synchronized-swimming star keeps telling herself. But as the first notes of "O Canada!" are played, tears stream down her face. "This moment will forever be engraved in my heart," she tells the adoring crowd.

That unforgettable moment crowns 18 years of battles waged more often against herself than her opponents, and of overcoming the tragedies that befell the 26-year-old woman.

Sylvie was two years old when she swam her first strokes at Montreal's Centre Immaculée Conception in 1969. She took instinctively to the water and loved every minute of it. At four, however, her world crumbled when her father, a city bus driver, was killed in a traffic accident.

Sylvie, her mother and younger brother moved into an apartment above her maternal grandparents' in the

Rosemont district of Montreal. Five years later, in 1974, Sylvie resumed swimming. Often, when she returned home from the pool, her grandfather, Ren Charbonneau, would be waiting for her at the bus stop at the top of their street. He always brought his dog, and on the way home he'd let his granddaughter hold the leash. "I was so proud," Sylvie recalls.

Sylvie proved very early to be an excellent swimmer. One afternoon she saw some young girls making figures in the water, turning in unison, arms reaching upward, as graceful as ballerinas. It was her first exposure to synchronized swimming, and it was love at first sight. One day, she promised herself, I'll be like them. She soon joined the Club Aquatique Montréal Olympique (CAMO).

In the spring of 1975, coach Julie Sauv welcomed her as a member of her beginners' team. She was struck by two things about Sylvie: her height — she was at least a head taller than the other girls her age — and her amazing flexibility.

"I must have been a dolphin in another life," Sylvie once joked to a friend. But as comfortable as she was in the water, outside her element she was shy and self-conscious. In school she was terrified at the thought of putting her hand up or talking in front of the class. And at the pool she would step into the background the moment she was out of the water. So, partly as a game, partly out of necessity, Sylvie invented an alter ego, someone more outgoing, whom she called Karine.

There were several other nine-year-old swimmers named Sylvie at CAMO. When Sauv gave instructions to one of them over the underwater speakers, all of them would correct their movement. To solve this, the girls decided to give themselves nicknames. When Sylvie Fréchette chose Karine, she felt transformed; suddenly she was self-confident, determined to win.

In 1979 Sylvie took part in the Junior Canadian Championships, her first national competition. She was

eliminated in the preliminaries, but that setback, far from demoralizing her, opened her eyes. *Some of them have more talent than I do,* she told herself, *so I'm just going to have to work harder.*

At 13 Sylvie began training 35 hours a week. She always swam after school, though, because her mother insisted that her education come first. "You'll never be able to make your living from swimming," she admonished Sylvie.

In synchronized swimming, artistic expression is as important as technique. When Sauv kept telling her, "You swim like a robot," Sylvie began practicing in front of the mirrors that lined the pool. Day after day she scrutinized and corrected her moves and sequences. She also, for eight hours a week, pulled 130-pound weights and executed scissors kicks with weights on her arms and legs.

To stay underwater for several minutes while executing figures that are precise to the hundredth of an inch, with every muscle crying out for oxygen, requires intensive training. The method consists of progressively increasing the time spent without breathing, as well as the number and difficulty of the movements. But Sylvie went even further. "Sometimes I hung on till I saw lights in front of my eyes, till I was two or three seconds from fainting," she says. Her determination paid off. She can stay underwater without moving for up to three minutes.

> *When Sauv kept telling her, "You swim like a robot," Sylvie began practicing in front of the mirrors that lined the pool.*

In 1984 Nathalie Audet from Quebec City became Sylvie's partner in duo events. From the start the two girls were very close. They didn't go out much with boys, were never home late on weekends and spent up to six hours a day at the pool. "We both desperately wanted to be champions," says Nathalie.

At the 1986 Canadian Championships, Sylvie and Nathalie came in second, but only the winners were eligible to compete in the world championships. With heavy hearts the pair broke up, and Sylvie decided to continue

on her own in singles. Her objective: the 1988 Olympics in Seoul.

Then came another blow. Although Sylvie was ranked No. 2 in Canada after Carolyn Waldo, sports authorities decided that Michelle Cameron, Waldo's partner, would go to Korea. It was a crushing disappointment for Sylvie. But her family rallied around her, especially her grandfather, who was always there for Sylvie's competitions in Montreal. "They helped me understand that I had to swim for myself," she says, "for my own pleasure, without worrying about judges or the swimming federation."

The new Sylvie soon created a sensation in the world of synchronized swimming. She swam to French songs, a novelty at the time, was bold enough not to smile at the judges, and she shed her austere swimsuits in favor of bold patterns and colors.

And she began to win top-level events. In 1986 she won the solo events at the Commonwealth Games in Edinburgh and the Moscow Invitational. In 1989 she brought home from the World Cup circuit three medals and vastly increased self-confidence. She also fell in love.

Sylvain Lake was a journalist with the French-language TV sports network Réseau des Sports (RDS) and a trackman who had competed in the 400 meters at the 1987 World University Games in Zagreb. They met in September 1989 in the RDS studios in Montreal where Lake interviewed her.

Sixteen months later, in January 1991, Sylvie was on her way to a major victory at the World Championships in Perth, Australia. She finished first in the compulsory figures, and if she did as well in the free figures, she would become champion. But she had an attack of stage fright and phoned Lake in Montreal. "I'm on my way," he told her.

It was a long journey from Montreal to Perth, but Lake managed to find a flight that would get him there one hour before the free figures were to start. Perfect, Sylvie thought, her self-confidence restored.

Not only did she walk away with the title, she got an unprecedented total of seven perfect scores of 10. That, despite the fact that Lake's plane was delayed and he arrived one hour after the event.

All that was left now was to bring home the gold from the next Olympics, in Barcelona; then she would retire because she and Lake had decided to get married.

But the Olympic year 1992 got off to the worst start imaginable. Sylvie's grandfather suffered a heart attack, and his death left a terrible void, a pain that only Lake's love helped to ease.

In the weeks leading up to the Olympics, as the stress and pressure of preparations built, the couple saw little of each other. On July 18, the day Lake was leaving for Barcelona as a track-and-field analyst for a television network, Sylvie had to present her Olympic program to the Canadian judge who would officiate at the Games, then go to a Montreal newspaper for a photo session.

She took stock of herself: I've lost the man I love. Swimming is all I have left. If I don't go to Barcelona, I've got nothing.

At breakfast Lake seemed depressed and uncommunicative. Sylvie knew that he sometimes went through such phases when he was tense. "I'll be back this afternoon to drive you to the airport," she told him. "That way we can have supper together, just the two of us."

But when Sylvie arrived home around three o'clock, she was met by the nauseating smell of exhaust gas. The car was running in the garage. She found Lake lying on the bed, asphyxiated. "I still don't understand why he did it," she says.

On July 21 Sylvie went to the morgue to identify Lake's body. She felt sick, so her mother took her to the doctor; Sylvie had an ulcer.

She took stock of herself: *I've lost the man I love. Swimming is all I have left. If I don't go to Barcelona, I've got nothing.*

During the preliminary trials in Barcelona, she tied for first place with American Kristen Babb-Sprague. Sylvie was disappointed. I'm the world champion, she thought. I have to do better.

August 5 was the date for the compulsory figures. Alone in the water, she executed four figures with absolute precision, never moving from her starting position despite wind and waves.

Leaving the pool, Sylvie was radiant. But what was going on? At the judges' table an argument was under way, and one judge seemed particularly upset. Sylvie didn't understand — until her points were displayed on the electronic board.

Four judges had given her scores between 9.2 and 9.6. But the fifth, Ana Maria da Silveira Lobo of Brazil, had erroneously typed 8.7 on her computer. She tried to correct the mistake, but it was too late. Her explanation did not persuade American referee Judy McGowan, who refused to change the score. The Canadians protested in vain. Sylvie was shattered; her chances for the gold medal had just disappeared. "If a truck is going to run over me," she told her mother, "let it come. I'm ready."

The free figures were still to come, but the gap in points was too great. *The only way I can win now*, Sylvie thought, *is if I walk on water. So I'm going to swim this program for all the sacrifices I've made over the past 18 years.*

> *At the judges' table an argument was under way, and one judge seemed particularly upset. Sylvie didn't understand — until her points were displayed on the electronic board.*

The following day she gave the most dazzling performance of her career. With five perfect scores of 10, she won hands down, but in the overall standings she was in second place.

The Canadian Amateur Synchronized Swimming Association did not let the matter rest, and continued to pressure Olympic authorities to rectify the injustice caused by a judge's slip of the finger.

Finally, on December 6, 1993, Sylvie received the news that she would get her gold medal (Babb-Sprague kept hers; they were officially declared co-winners). At last she could savor her victory. On the Quebec TV show "Ad Lib" a few days later, Sylvie handed her silver medal to a mailman who, with hundreds of thousands of viewers looking on, wrapped it up to be sent back to the International Olympic Committee.

Since then, the once-bashful young woman has hosted a TV show, launched her own line of bathing suits and taken up a new challenge: encouraging kids to stay in school.

"Hello," she says in a typical meeting with 500 students at a Montreal high school, "my name is Sylvie Fréchette." The students stop talking. They listen. To a simple message, a true story. "I've come here to share a side of myself that you don't know about. I've come to tell you how a dream can come true."

That dream is shining brightly again. On November 30, 1994, Sylvie announced she was coming out of retirement to seek Olympic gold in Atlanta in 1996. "Call it unfinished business," she says.

Despite some opposition from some Canadian athletes who called her "selfish" for returning to the sport and not letting younger athletes get a chance to compete, Sylvie qualified to head the 1996 Canadian Olympic synchronized swimming team. Sylvie's autobiography, Gold at Last (Stoddart), was published in December, 1994. In this book she describes her life experiences leading to her being awarded the gold medal for her performance at the Barcelona Olympics.

WINNERS FOR LIFE

by Eugene H. Methvin

Year after year Coach Bob Shannon takes undisciplined youths — and turns them into proud young adults with a chance.

BOB SHANNON, coach of the East St. Louis, Ill., High School football team, had a problem. His unbelievably talented quarterback prospect, James Harris, had skipped the Flyers' off-season work-outs, seeming to feel his raw talent would prevail. Six-feet-eight-inches tall, weighing 210 pounds, Harris had a bazooka for an arm and could run.

But Shannon always expected his quarterbacks to set an example of self-discipline and sacrifice both on and off the field. So, even though the coach had no idea who could substitute for Harris, he laid down the law to his player: "You're not going to play quarterback. If you play at all, it will be catching passes, not throwing them."

The angry youngster transferred to the Flyers' rival, Lincoln High, and Shannon drafted a gritty running back,

Kerwin Price, to take over the signal-calling. Several weeks later, when the two teams met, the Flyers crushed their rival 61–7. "We stuck to our principles," Shannon said. "Now we see it's team, not talent, that counts most." The Flyers went on to an undefeated season, winning recognition as the nation's No. 1 high-school football team.

Gideon's Army. Shannon's teams are a beacon of excellence in one of the nation's worst sinkholes of social decay. Crime and violence swirl around the coach and his team. One morning they found the body of an executed drug dealer on their practice field. On several occasions, they have had to hit the turf when gun battles erupted on adjacent streets.

East St. Louis, abandoned by industry, has lost half its population in the last three decades. Shannon estimates that 60 percent of his players come from single-parent homes, and 80 percent receive public assistance. Because of a dwindling tax base, the school board has had financial troubles in recent years, and Shannon has had to dig into his own pocket to buy athletic equipment.

Despite such handicaps, every year Shannon, like the Old Testament's Gideon, recruits a tiny band of faithful and valiant warriors who respond to his tough demands and trample their opponents. In the past 12 years they have won five Illinois state championships.

Declares St. Louis *Post-Dispatch* sportswriter Mike Eisenbath: "Shannon's great achievement has been to take undisciplined youths with little hope and turn them into proud young men with a chance."

Shannon does this by giving his players the lessons he learned in his own climb up from a harsh childhood in Natchez, Miss. He was the second of 12 children of parents who had no schooling beyond third grade. His father, disabled by asthma, died when Bob was 12. The family survived on Social Security and the $10 a week his mother earned as a domestic.

Every day the boy walked five miles from their tin-roofed shanty to the nearest school for black children. Both education and sports became his passion. He quarterbacked his high school to its first undefeated season ever.

He also was promising enough as a baseball player that the Pittsburgh Pirates drafted him out of high school, dangling an $8,000 bonus to sign. Instead, Shannon went to Tennessee State University on a football scholarship, where his offensive coach was a Bible-quoting disciplinarian named "Cat" Coleman. "More important than how to play football," Coleman told his players, "is how to set goals and pay the price to achieve them. I can't do it for you. Like Jesus' disciples, you've got to go out there and bring my words to life."

One afternoon, some older players, disgruntled with

the program, plotted a strike. When summoned to scrimmage, they decided, everybody would simply leave the field. Shannon said nothing. But when the whistle blew, he jogged toward the practice field as usual. "What are you doing, Bob?" the protesters called. Over his shoulder, Shannon answered, "I forgot to tell you — I'm a disciple!" His teammates hesitated and then fell in behind him. The strike was over.

The Washington Redskins drafted Shannon in 1969, and he made it through training camp before becoming one of the last prospects cut. Though the Atlanta Falcons offered him a contract, Shannon decided to marry his college sweetheart, Jeanette Ridley, and get on with his chosen career of teaching and coaching.

Told about an opening for an assistant football coach in East St. Louis, Shannon went for an interview. He was dismayed when he saw the deteriorating city — filthy streets, boarded-up buildings and overgrown vacant lots. Even in its poorest sections, Natchez was well kept. But he landed the job and looked forward to the challenge ahead.

"Talent without discipline is meaningless. The streets are full of guys talking about how good they were, clutching a bottle in their hands."

Straight Talk. For five years, Shannon remained an assistant coach. But in 1976, following a winless season for the Flyers, he was tapped to become the new head coach. Shannon promptly let everyone know a new day had arrived. He kicked three players off the squad for skipping practice. The principal, pressured by parents, ordered them reinstated. "You're the boss, but I'm the coach — and I don't have to play them!" Shannon declared. He told his squad, "Talent without discipline is meaningless. The streets are full of guys talking about how good they were, clutching a bottle in their hands."

The new coach had a severe "no pass–no play" rule. If a player needed help with his studies, Shannon would find him a tutor, preferably a pretty female student to help with his motivation. But if the player was simply not working, he got bounced from the team. And woe to the athlete who caused trouble in class. "You can't be a good player and a bad citizen," Shannon ruled.

Many a mother also found the coach on her side. One day, while studying films with his team, he interrupted to instruct a player, "Kevin, get home and paint that porch like your mama told you." Kevin Ramsey turned into a star, winning, with Shannon's help, a scholarship to Indiana State.

Today an assistant coach at Northwestern University, Ramsey regularly talks with his old coach. "He tells me not what I want to hear but what I *need* to hear."

Within two years, the Flyers made the state play-offs. However, in the semifinal contest, one of Chicago's perennial football powers, St. Rita, walloped them 48–13. After the game, Shannon told his players, "They did us a favor by showing us what *good* is. That's going to be our measuring stick from now on."

Shannon discovered that St. Rita's players employed a year-round weight-lifting program to build strength. He launched one too. In their summer camp the Flyers began practicing three times a day. Kerry Glenn, now a Miami Dolphins cornerback, says, "He had us doing things in high school I'm doing now in the pros."

At a parents' meeting Shannon explained, "We don't have the advantages others have. But we have pride and commitment to the word *excellence*, which is second to none." He sat down to resounding applause.

Winning at Life. In 1979, four years after taking over a winless team, Shannon's Flyers won the state championship. "The Streak" — 44 straight victories, including three more state championships — began in September 1983. The school's weed-studded practice field and dilapidated stadium became a mecca for reporters. Yet Shannon forbade his players to talk about the victory string. "Focus on streaking and we'll forget to play football," he warned. Before each game, the Flyers continued to kneel while one player recited a prayer: "We ask for a chance to strike . . . and if we should lose, to stand by the side and cheer as the winner goes by."

In October 1986, the Flyers finally stood by and

cheered another team — Granite City. Shannon had often told his players, "I'd rather lose with mediocre guys than win with a talented bad guy." The week of the Granite City game, everybody found out he meant it. For disciplinary reasons Shannon benched three key players, even though the squad was injury-riddled. Then, on the game's opening drive, the Flyers' leading ball carrier was hurt. Still, Shannon refused to call on the "bad guys." That afternoon The Streak ended, 17–14.

In 1988 Shannon suspended his most talented pass receiver, Kenny Dunn, for missing practice and "hanging out with the wrong crowd." Dunn listened on the radio as his teammates lost the state title. As always, Shannon made no apologies: "Our kids have to win more than just a football game. They have to win at the game of life."

Many on the squad played that championship game with pants so tattered that their skin showed through. The coach told them, "We've got nothing to be ashamed of. Life isn't always fair, but we can still expect excellence from ourselves."

St. Louis *Post-Dispatch* sports editor Kevin Horrigan wrote: "This is a story Hollywood wouldn't believe: kids growing up in America's biggest urban disaster, slugging it out, year after year. No money, no fancy facilities, just a coach who still believes pride and hard work can mean something." St. Louis businessmen promptly chipped in to buy the team new uniforms.

During the 1989 season, the Flyers rolled over nine regular-season opponents on the way to the playoffs by the combined score of 410–80. Trouble came, however, in the state quarter-finals. The Carl Sandburg High Eagles were tough, and, with the clock running out, the Flyers trailed 13–7. Then quarterback Rollie Nevilles took over, leading the Flyers to the Sandburg five-yard line. Finally it came down to fourth and goal to go — their last chance.

The year before, Kenny Dunn had listened on the radio as his team lost the championship without him. This season he had been first on the field for every practice. Nevilles took the snap, rolled out, then threw to

Dunn in the end zone. Dunn made the catch, and the Flyers won 14–13.

When they filed into the dressing room, their elation turned to shock and anger. Someone had ransacked their lockers and stolen their money and personal items. The coach commanded, "Let's get down on our knees, fellows." The whole team recited the Lord's Prayer, as they do after every game. Then Shannon, with a gesture to the pillaged lockers, said, "When we say, 'Forgive us our trespasses as we forgive those who trespass against us,' this is what we mean. Now let's get on our bus and go home." Two weeks later, Shannon's Flyers won the state championship 55–8.

In 1990, the team extended its winning streak to 26 games before losing in the state semifinal. After the game Shannon told his players, "Winning is not the only thing. You gave your best effort and can be proud of it all your life."

Inevitably, journalists ask Shannon how he can achieve excellence in the middle of "America's biggest urban disaster." His answer: "We battle tough odds. But we don't look for excuses to explain failure. We look for ways to succeed."

> *"We battle tough odds. But we don't look for excuses to explain failure. We look for ways to succeed."*

Former players come to see their old coach and encourage current players to stick it out. Shannon's alumni follow a solemn commission the coach lays on each departing player: "Pass along the lessons you've learned to somebody else. It's a debt you owe to those who've helped you." Says ex-Flyer Craig Patton, a manager at J. C. Penney, "I have a 12-year-old son, and I tell him some of my beliefs that I've learned from Coach Shannon."

Years ago, after the first Illinois championship, Shannon began to receive a steady stream of job offers. He turned them all down. One of his players, the Miami Dolphins' Kerry Glenn, asked why. Shannon's answer: "I'd rather work with the kids of East St. Louis. If I don't care about them, who will?"

WHAT MAKES OLYMPIC CHAMPIONS?

By John E. Anderson

It's not just athletic skill that molds winners: here are seven traits that distinguish the best of the best.

WHEN KRISTI YAMAGUCHI fell to the ice in the 1992 Winter Olympics at Albertville, France, spectators groaned. Surely the 20-year-old's chances for a gold medal in figure skating had evaporated with that tumble. But Kristi scrambled up, flashed a dazzling smile and spun back into her program. When the judges' scores were announced, she had received near-perfect marks despite the spill. Her spirited recovery gave her the gold medal — a tribute to her determination and courage.

As a consultant to U.S. Olympic teams and many individual athletes, I've seen dozens of young men and women like Kristi who reached deep into themselves at a critical moment and found something that brought out their best. They mounted the winners' stand not simply because of athletic talent but because of resolute inner fiber.

Indeed, at a world-class competition like the Winter Olympics in Lillehammer, Norway, there's only an infinitesimal difference in athletic ability between No. 1 and No. 2. What counts is what goes on between the ears. Diann Roffe-Steinrotter, the U.S. ski team's silver medalist in the giant slalom in 1992, may have said it best: "If you're not strong mentally and don't

> ... there's only an infinistesimal difference ... between No. 1 and No. 2. What counts is what goes on between the ears.

know how to make sacrifices, you don't have a chance."

Over the years I've pinpointed several qualities that make Olympic champions. These characteristics are invaluable wherever they are applied — in school, in the home or on the job:

They had a dream.

Kristi Yamaguchi visualized herself as an Olympic champion the first time she put on skates, at age six. Bonny Warner, who represented the United States in three Olympic luge competitions, didn't have her dream until she was a college student. Before that, she had never heard of the racing sled called a luge. But once the dream took shape, both young women clung to it tenaciously and worked to make it come true.

Most important, their parents and those around them supported the dream. Loretta Dawes, whose 16-year-old daughter, Dominique, was one of the first female black gymnasts to represent the United States in the Olympics, recently told the press that bringing up a world-class athlete isn't easy. For an entire year before the 1992 Olympics, she rarely saw her daughter, who lived with her coach to be closer to the gym, a 45-minute drive from home. Dawes was asked what advice she would give other parents of athletes. She answered simply and eloquently. "Believe in your child," she said.

. . . being able to dream is the first step on every road to success — even if the initial dream eventually leads to a different road.

That doesn't mean every child who dreams of Olympic fame will one day climb onto the winners' stand. But being able to dream is the first step on every road to success — even if the initial dream eventually leads to a different road. The Rev. Jesse Jackson, for example, once considered a career as a professional baseball player. However, he channeled his ability to dream in other directions.

They're fired up.

The Olympic flame that top performers pursue burns inside them. They're driven not only to *be* the best but to *do* their best — always.

That's why Carl Lewis, who already holds eight Olympic gold medals, planned to compete again at 36 in the 1996 Games, against youngsters half his age; and why discus thrower Al Oerter, after winning gold medals in

Kristi Yamaguchi
On the ice in the 1992 World Figure Skating

four consecutive Olympics, tried again for the Olympic team at age 47.

Swimmer Janet Evans, who won three gold medals in Seoul in 1988, embodied that same desire to win four years later. After she narrowly missed a gold medal in the 400-meter freestyle, she swam one of the most psychologically challenging races of her life in the 800-meter freestyle to win the gold. "I just wanted to be up there on that winners' stand one more time," she confessed. The class valedictorian, the corporate CEO — those who rise to the top in any endeavor — must have that same drive.

They bounce back.

Television coverage focuses on victories, but the Olympics are also about defeat. In the 1992 men's giant slalom, for instance, there were three medalists — and 130 other skiers who didn't get medals. Athletes know that losing is part of what they do. Real winners in sports, as in business or school, are those whose failures inspire them to go at it again.

> *In setting our sights low, we often live up to our expectations.*

Swimmer Mike Barrowman used to wear his second- and third-place medals to bed to make himself think about what he might have done differently to finish first. His method paid off. He won the 200-meter breast-stroke in world-record time in 1992.

They aim high.

I once asked a world-class athlete to guess at the outcome of a major competition. "I'll come in fifth," he said. And that's exactly where he finished, even though he could easily have placed third, or even second, since two other major contenders fared poorly. In setting our sights low, we often live up to our expectations.

Contrast him with "Flo Jo" — Florence Griffith-Joyner. Training a week before the 1988 Games, she wrote in her diary the time she expected to run and win the

100-meter dash: 10.54 seconds. When Flo Jo crossed the finish line, the clock showed 10.54. She had not only seen herself winning, but called her winning time to the split second.

They plan for trouble.

In the 1984 Olympics, heavyweight boxer Henry Tillman laid out a careful strategy. He would fight defensively, warding off his opponent's blows while waiting for an opening. But when the bout began, it became obvious that the other fighter had decided to do the same thing. After the first round, Tillman stepped back and dropped his hands; you could almost see him mentally shift gears. Knowing his initial game plan might not work, he had come prepared with a second. He switched to the offensive, and he won the match — and ultimately a gold medal.

An inner dynamo keeps Olympic champions going — not just the promise of a medal, but the satisfaction of completing a difficult task against the odds.

Kristi Yamaguchi was ready too. Originally, after the move that made her stumble, she had planned to perform her most difficult jump — three revolutions in the air and a graceful single-skate landing known as a triple salchow. But Kristi was ready with a substitute in case she erred. She cut the triple salchow to a double, enabling her to regain her balance and rhythm and catch up with her music. Then she went on to perform another triple jump, the lutz. Her performance was flawless thereafter.

No matter how much we rehearse, things don't always work out according to plan. The true champion, in sports or elsewhere, anticipates possible setbacks and prepares for them.

They never quit.

The 1992 Summer Olympics featured two tremendously poignant moments. American sprinter Gail Devers, the clear leader in the 100-meter hurdles, tripped over the last barrier. She agonizingly pulled herself to her knees and crawled the last five meters, finishing fifth — but finishing.

Even more heart-rending was the 400-meter semifinal in which British runner Derek Redmond tore a hamstring and fell to the track. He struggled to his feet and began to hobble, determined to complete the race. His father ran from the stands to help him off the track, but the athlete refused to quit. He leaned on his father, and the two limped to the finish line together, to deafening applause.

Hanging in there despite setbacks teaches us the value of perseverance. An inner dynamo keeps Olympic champions going — not just the promise of a medal, but the satisfaction of completing a difficult task against the odds. That same effort can apply whether the task is a race, a difficult mathematics lesson or a corporate report.

They make their own luck.
When Paul Wylie won a silver medal in men's figure skating at Albertville, he surprised everyone but himself. Several skaters who had been expected to win medals had been injured or had performed poorly. "I was the last person expected to make the winners' podium," Wylie said. "But I had trained like crazy, and when the favorites faltered, I was ready."

Month after month, year after year, Olympians I know go through a grind of pointing toward their big moment. Skaters arise at 4 A.M. to squeeze in a few hours of practice before a rink is open to the public. Cyclists put in hours of roadwork before reporting to their daily jobs. Boxers head for the gym and work out relentlessly every day.

In the Olympics, as in other aspects of life, luck certainly counts. The second clarinetist who has practiced diligently is lucky to get a chance to solo when the first clarinetist becomes ill. So is the assistant sales manager

who fills in for the boss in an emergency. But both must be well prepared for their big break. When others slipped, Wylie stepped in and skated perfectly. In the Olympics — in everything — luck strikes those prepared to capitalize on it.

As you watch the next Winter Olympics, look beyond the skaters' leaps and loops, the skiers slicing around slalom gates, the two-man and four-man bobsleds roaring down the course. In these spectacular maneuvers and superb performances, you can see qualities less easily measurable — qualities we can learn from, qualities for our children to imitate.

UNFORGETTABLE FRED LEBOW

by Grete Waitz

**He turned an obscure local running event
into the world's most famous marathon.**

I can still see Fred at the starting line that warm
October morning in 1978. Hopping up and down,
bellowing into his megaphone, the 46-year-old
maestro barked endless orders at a sea of runners.
They were lining up for the ninth annual New York City
Marathon, and Fred Lebow's bearded face glowed with
excitement.

It was my first visit to the United States and my first
marathon. Twenty-five years old, I had represented
Norway in the 1,500-meter event at the 1972 and 1976
Olympics, and set a 1975 world record in a 3,000-meter
race. I was a track runner used to short distances — a
mile or so — with 10 or 12 competitors at most.

Now, feeling overwhelmed, I swallowed hard and
looked at the 9,875 runners lining up at the Verrazano-

Narrows Bridge that sweeps across New York Harbor.
I thought of the 26.2-mile course that stretched before
me, winding through all five New York boroughs to
the finish line in Central Park. *Can I really run that far?*
I asked myself.

I looked again at Fred. He knew I was a short-distance runner. Yet, sight unseen, he believed enough in
me to fly my husband, Jack, and me to the United States
from Norway so I could try this unique race.

Fred had dismissed the fact that I'd retired from
competitive sports to become a schoolteacher, and that
I'd never even run a marathon before. "You have a
worldwide reputation as a top runner," he argued when
he called me in Oslo. "It doesn't matter that you're a
short-distance champion. I want more women to enter,
and you'll be a drawing card. I want this to be a race
for everybody."

Okay, Fred, I thought, lacing my shoes. *I'll give it my
best.* Two hours and 32 minutes later, I crossed the
finish line in Central Park. In the unseasonable 75-
degree heat, feeling suffocated with my clothes clinging to
my body, I pulled off my running shoes and threw them
at Jack. "I'm never going to run this distance again," I
vowed. Only when reporters asked how it felt to be
No. I did I realize I'd won the women's division and set a
new world record. My surprising triumph marked the
beginning of a 16-year friendship that changed the
course of my life—the same way Fred changed many
other lives as well.

The next year, I won the marathon again, breaking my
own previous record. By 1980 I had quit teaching to run
long road races full time, and I went on to win nine New
York marathons—all because of Fred.

To Fred Lebow, marathons weren't just about running
—they were about life. "In running," he told me, "it
doesn't matter whether you come in first or last. What's
important is being able to say, 'I finished!'" It was Fred's
mission to see that as many people as possible shared in
that special satisfaction of "finishing." Some races, like the
Boston Marathon, exclude runners who haven't qualified
by doing well in a previous event. From the start Fred

insisted that his race be open to everyone age 18 and up, no matter what his or her abilities happened to be. He wanted the New York City Marathon to be a people's race.

"The beauty of my race," he often said, "is that amateurs run with world-class athletes. That's something you don't find anywhere else. I can't compete in a tennis match with a pro," he'd say with his infectious grin, "but I can run in the New York marathon with world champions like Grete Waitz."

Through the sheer force of his personality, this human dynamo turned an obscure local running event into one of the world's biggest single athletic happenings.

"Always a Winner." Fred Lebow (pronounced LEE-boh) was born Fischl Lebowitz in Arad, Romania, on June 3, 1932. The sixth of seven children in a Jewish family, the young boy had a happy childhood. Then came World War II. When the Nazis took power in Romania, the Lebowitzes and other Jewish families lived in fear for their lives. In the final battle for Romania, the Soviet army defeated the Germans, leading to the Soviet Communist takeover. In 1947 Fred and an older brother fled to Czechoslovakia.

... he loved the freedom of putting on his shoes and heading out the door, the sensation of the earth slipping beneath his feet.

The two arrived in the United States in 1949, unable to speak English. Fred shortened his name to Lebow and wound up in New York City, enrolling at the Fashion Institute of Technology. He soon made a successful career creating and selling copies of designer clothing that the ordinary person could afford.

An avid tennis player, Fred was often frustrated by how quickly he ran out of steam — and how often he lost. When a doctor suggested running as a way to build stamina, Fred began with a slow trot around the Central Park reservoir. Immediately he loved the freedom of putting on his shoes and heading out the door, the sensation of the earth slipping beneath his feet. He was hooked.

"Running is the only sport of its kind," he told me. "You compete against yourself and can always do better in the next race, so you're always a winner."

Fred loved telling the story of the first official race he ever entered — a five-mile event — when he was 39. "I crossed the finish line second to last — just ahead of a 72-year-old man. I owe him a favor because if I'd come in last that day, I would have given up running for good."

In 1970 Fred joined the New York Road Runners Club and supplied $300 in seed money for the organization's first marathon — a casual affair consisting of four loops around Central Park. Of the 127 who started, 55 crossed the finish line. Fred was 44th.

Elected club president in 1972, Fred decided to devote himself full time to running. He'd made a comfortable living in the garment industry, but money wasn't an important part of his life — running was.

He was delighted when, under his leadership, the marathon spread to the five boroughs and eventually included more than 28,000 participants. He loved the idea of his runners — hailing from Afghanistan to Zimbabwe — passing through so many ethnic neighborhoods. It fit his image of the marathon as a unifying race for all.

> *He loved the idea of his runners — hailing from Afghanistan to Zimbabwe — passing through so many ethnic neighborhoods. It fit his image of the marathon ...*

Cheering Section. To keep his runners pumped up during races, Fred always rode in an open convertible that preceded the front runners. Then, all along the route, he would shout through his bullhorn at people in their apartments, offices and shops: "Here come the runners! Come out and give them a hand!"

Recruiting a cheering section wasn't always easy, however. He once told me about the time four burly, angry teens marched into the Road Runners Club, demanding to see the president. They hailed from a rough section of the city and didn't want the runners invading their turf. They told Fred he'd better back off.

Typically, Fred saw an opportunity here. "This is wonderful!" he told them. "We need someone to protect the runners in your area, and you look like just the fellows to do it." He passed out caps, jackets and T-shirts emblazoned with the Road Runners logo. On race day, the gang members stood proudly along the streets of their turf, wearing the gear he'd given them.

Whenever I spotted Fred at the finish line, it was like a shot of adrenalin. His face beaming, his arms rotating like windmills, he could always hurry me and the others to finish just a bit faster. Then, after the winners had crossed the line, he would be back to welcome the later runners, shouting encouragement for them to hurry too. Fred also arranged for everyone who completed the race to get a medal.

One year, two days after the marathon, Fred got a call that a runner was still out. A Vietnam veteran who had lost his legs was covering the distance by swinging himself forward on his hands. Fred searched the route and finally found the man in the Bronx. It took the vet two more days to complete the race, and Fred kept coming out to see how he was doing. When the man finally approached the finish line, Fred was there waving his arms in encouragement.

Once his marathon spread to the five boroughs, Fred was too busy organizing the race to compete in it. But he did run in others — ultimately 69 in 30 countries. With his spindly legs and slow, awkward gait, he usually finished near the end of the pack, but that was fine with him. It was crossing the line that mattered, not winning.

Gloomy Prognosis. In January 1990, Fred started slurring his words. Soon he began forgetting the names of close friends and co-workers. An MRI and biopsy revealed a malignant tumor in the left frontal lobe of his brain. Doctors gave him six months to live — a prognosis Fred refused to accept. Months of chemotherapy and radiation followed. When the therapy made Fred too weak to get out of bed, he did isometric exercises with his hands and legs. As soon as he regained enough strength, he walked the hospital corridors. Before long, a small band of patients was trooping behind him.

When Fred was discharged, he returned to Central Park for his afternoon runs, but his pace was only half what it had been. Determined to do better, Fred cajoled his buddy and second-in-command at the Road Runners Club, Allan Steinfeld, to train with him.

As Fred chugged doggedly around Central Park's reservoir, his trademark bicycle cap covering a head made bald from chemotherapy, Allan ran backward in front of him, shouting encouragement and advice.

Fred fought back hard, and the tumor shrank. Doctors pronounced him in remission. Then, in the spring of 1992, he dropped a bombshell. "Grete," he announced, "this fall I'm going to run in my own marathon again. If I can do this, I'll know I've beaten the disease." He asked if I'd help him train.

"On one condition," I said. "You let me run this one alongside you."

On Marathon Day 1992, Fred and I eagerly joined the other runners at the rear of the pack on the Staten Island side of the Verrazano bridge.

There are always hundreds of thousands of spectators along the route, but I'd never been more aware of them than I was that day. Everywhere people shouted, waved and cheered us on. "We love you, Fred!" they yelled, their voices tight with emotion. Near Memorial Sloan-Kettering Cancer Center, where Fred had received treatment, staff and patients lined the sidewalks. Some of the patients were children battling cancer. "Go Fred!" they shouted in thin voices. "Do it for us!"

About five miles from the finish, Fred seemed to run out of steam. We rested a minute, and then continued at a slow shuffle. As we entered Central Park, he perked up like a horse heading home to stable. This was Fred's park, where he first started running, where he'd begun his marathon. The emotional rush brought goose bumps to my arms, and I started to cry.

Fred looked alarmed. "Grete, are you hurting? What's wrong?" he asked.

"I'm just happy we're going to make it," I said. And then he started to cry too. We ran the last two miles side by side, holding hands, both of us in tears.

As we crossed the finish line, 5½ hours after we had started, several thousand people roared in a standing ovation. Fred sank to his knees and kissed the ground. He'd fulfilled his dream in dignity and style. He'd finished.

"What Have I Done?" After I returned to Norway, Fred and I kept in touch often. Then, in the fall of last year, I received a dreaded phone call from the Road Runners Club: "Grete, you'd better come to New York. Fred is very sick."

Jack and I caught a plane, and we went to Fred's apartment. In a faint voice, he told me about a life-size bronze statue a friend and former runner had commissioned. "It shows me in my running suit and cap looking down at my watch as if checking a runner's time. The statue's going to be placed at the finish line in time for this year's marathon." Fred said he felt embarrassed. "What have I done to deserve a statue?"

"Everything," I answered, taking his hand. "For me —and for tens of thousands of others."

On Sunday, October 9, 1994, Fred Lebow, the legendary Marathon Man, died peacefully in his sleep at age 62. After a private family ceremony, the funeral procession drove to the marathon finish line in Central Park. Then the entourage drove slowly past the Road Runners Club and out to a cemetery near Shea Stadium, where Fred was buried. At his memorial service in Central Park the following Wednesday, almost 4,000 people attended — the wealthy and the poor, the famous and the unknown. They all had one thing in common: a deep affection for Fred Lebow.

> *"Fate handed him a short race.*
>
> *With his gall, with his love of life, Fred*
>
> *Lebow turned it into a marathon."*

Every year, the New York marathon is held in November. The race, the thousands of men and women who run it, and the hundreds of thousands more who cheer them on each year will forever be Fred's living legacy. Sportswriter George Vecsey put it best: "Fate handed him a short race. With his gall, with his love of life, Fred Lebow turned it into a marathon."

JIMMIE HEUGA: TWICE A CHAMPION

by Jack Fincher

When multiple sclerosis struck this former Olympic skiing medalist, he needed all the courage he could muster to hit back, to live as he had competed — all out.

JIMMIE HEUGA just lay there, too weak to move. At 32, he was divorced, alone and employed in an unfulfilling job. He felt trapped, helpless, boxed in by his diseased body. Outside he could see people jogging, playing touch football, water-skiing on Long Island Sound — all things "Shakes" Heuga (as friends now called him) could no longer do.

Although it was a sparkling spring day, torpor hung upon Jimmie's compact frame like a suit of armor. *I'm about as close to a wheelchair as you can get,* he thought. In his budding fear, he sensed seeds of panic — like grains of blowing snow that become an avalanche.

As he stared at the ceiling of his one-room cottage by the Connecticut shore, Jimmie's thoughts drifted back a dozen years to the 1964 Winter Olympics in Innsbruck, Austria. He remembered the steep slalom course, made icy and treacherous by the earlier runs of a dozen skiers. How amazed everyone had been when Jimmie had challenged his fear, skidding and flashing through the zigzag run of gates to win the bronze medal.

Flushed with triumph, Jimmie Heuga, 20, had joined his silver-medal-winning teammate Billy Kidd to pose as America's first-ever Olympic medalists in men's alpine skiing. It had been a heady moment for the likable little Californian with the curly black hair and flashing smile.

"*Hew-gah*, not *Waygah*," reporters corrected one another. "Basque, not Spanish." Jimmie was now someone to be reckoned with in ski racing.

"Just Tired." At the 1968 Winter Olympics in Grenoble, France, Jimmie, about to be married and fresh from a third-place giant-slalom finish in the 1967 World Cup races, did badly. His coordination and timing seemed off. Still, at the Olympics you didn't fuss; you skied. He had been racing since he was five, back in Squaw Valley where his father had worked as a lift operator. *This is just burnout*, Jimmie thought. *I'm just tired.*

It was another year before he went to a Colorado neurologist with worsening symptoms — tingling from the waist down, blurred vision, distorted depth perception. The neurologist put him through a series of tests, then told him, "I think you have multiple sclerosis." Jimmie was stunned. *Yesterday I ran five miles in 25 minutes, he thought. How can I be sick?*

When a spinal tap confirmed the diagnosis, Jimmie's neurologist explained the disease, a mysterious, unpredictable malady that afflicts an estimated 250,000 Americans: "MS destroys the myelin sheath, a fatty membrane that covers nerve fibers, leaving scar tissue in its place. The lesions cause certain electrochemical nerve impulses coursing through your body to 'short out,' and this disrupts body functions: muscle movement, balance, strength, coordination, bladder control, sexual potency, speech, vision, touch." Believed to involve an immune-system defect, a slow-acting virus or both, MS tends to be progressive. It is also incurable, and sometimes leads to life in a wheelchair.

Jimmie should avoid stress but stay active, the doctor went on. In the frequent episodes of overwhelming lassitude that characterize the disease, many patients seem all too willing to retire to the sidelines. Just the

> *At the 1968 Winter Olympics in Grenoble, France, Jimmie ... did badly. His coordination and timing seemed off.*

same, too much exertion could be harmful. "Think of your energy as capital," the doctor concluded. "All of us have only so much to invest, and MS patients far less than most. You don't want to exhaust yourself."

In 1972 a dejected Jimmie hardly watched the Winter Olympics on television. His marriage had ended; his disease was progressing; the two sports stores in which he had an interest were failing. During the next few years, he sank steadily. He could no longer ski, or even run. On hot days, he could barely walk.

Head-On Attack. In the spring of 1976, as he lay in that Connecticut cottage — unable or unwilling to rise — he thought things over. There was no getting around it: MS was turning him into a parody of the world-class athlete he had once been. What had he told reporters after winning the bronze? "When I'm on the ropes," he had said, "that's when I'm at my best." *Well,* Jimmie thought, *I'm on the ropes now. What do I do about it?*

Suddenly, he saw, propped against the wall, his English racing bike. If he worked his feet into the pedal straps, could he sustain his balance and get up sufficient speed to shake his lethargy?

Jimmie eased out of bed and reeled outside. Pushing the bike down to a fence, he leaned against it and mounted unsteadily. He pushed off, coasting slowly down the gentle hill. He traveled 100 yards before he lost his balance and fell.

No matter! Jimmie felt the exhilarating presence of an old ally: fatigue from exercise. The fatigue and sweat made him remember how good it felt to be fully alive.

Staggering to his feet, he tried the bike again. And again.

That night Jimmie knew that he was through denying the disease's subtle onslaught, through enduring its insidious effects as it robbed him of what made life worthwhile. From now on he would live as he had competed: by hitting back, attacking his tormentor as he had the slalom course — all out and head on.

Dubious Doctor. For a while he had trouble even getting on his bicycle, but Jimmie was soon cycling 25 miles a week and doing 50 pushups a day. He moved back to Colorado and, before long, he felt ready to confront his biggest challenge: to resume skiing.

At first it took all his energy just to get his boots and skis on. There were times he could summon only enough strength to slide down the mountain sitting on his skis. But by 1980, when he accepted a job representing a ski-and-sportswear company in California, Jimmie was able to ski jerkily down beginner slopes.

At a ski-equipment show, he ran into an old friend, motion-picture producer Warren Miller. When Miller heard that Jimmie was back on skis, he said, "I'd like to film that." Jimmie agreed to cooperate. Afterward, Jimmie showed the movie to his doctor, Labe Scheinberg, and then to Scheinberg's MS patients at Albert Einstein College of Medicine in New York City. Most of them were in advanced stages of the disease, and Jimmie could see the doubt in their eyes: *They weren't former Olympic athletes.*

Scheinberg himself was dubious about Jimmie's regimen. Jimmie pressed him. Were there any signs that the calisthenics and biking were damaging him? Scheinberg admitted there were not. "Then it's a risk I have to take," Jimmie said, "if it means living the life I want to live."

By 1981 Jimmie had set his sights on a higher goal: imparting his belief in living life to the fullest to others with MS. His employer gave him a leave of absence, and the National Multiple Sclerosis Society offered to help with expenses. Dr. Scheinberg was skeptical. "Jimmie," he said, "I see what you're doing, and maybe it works for you. But I can't advocate this approach for other patients."

"I'm not suggesting that people in wheelchairs do

> *At first it took all his energy just to get his boots and skis on. There were times he could summon only enough strength to slide down the mountain sitting on his skis.*

exactly what I do," Jimmie responded. "What I'm saying is that they find the motivation to live their lives as fully as possible. Painters should paint; knitters should knit. But first they've got to get in good enough physical shape to feel like doing it."

Later that year, at a fund-raising banquet for the New York City chapter of the Multiple Sclerosis Society, Jimmie was honored with The Special Achievement Award. Labe Scheinberg said to Jimmie, "A lot of my patients are sitting out there in wheelchairs. And you know something, Jimmie? Many of them have a lot less nerve damage than you do."

"It Works!" Today Jimmie Heuga travels thousands of miles a year for the National Multiple Sclerosis Society, participating in bike-a-thons and other benefit events and boosting the value of exercise, as he did one Saturday morning last October in Omaha. More than 100 people with MS and their families had gathered in a downtown church. Carrying a brass-knobbed walking stick and wearing a jaunty blue beret, Jimmie made his way to the podium with the stiff-legged gait that often leads strangers to suspect that he has been drinking.

He began by sharing his memory of that awful after-noon in Connecticut. "The less I did, the less I wanted to do — and the less I *could* do," he said. "Treat your MS like a challenge," he advised. "Animate yourself. The quality of your life, that's what's important. Stay in as good condition as you can. Forget about others; compete with *yourself.*

"The 'beast' is not the physical effects of the disease," Jimmie added. "It's the loss of self-esteem and self-confidence that can come with it. Remember, everyone has a crutch, a cross to bear. If my MS were cured tomorrow, it would not change the quality of my life. I decided to exercise, to take charge, and *that* changed my life. I would not trade now with anyone on earth."

Later, people asked: Has your MS improved? Jimmie's reply: "The nerve damage is still there, of course, but I

just try to make the most of what I have. Some days are diamond; some days are stone. Sometimes I still have to crawl around on my hands and knees. So I set realistic goals that allow for lapses. I take each day as a challenge. You can too."

Then Jimmie invited his astonished listeners to attend a free pilot program he was offering in Vail, Colo. There, last January, a team of neurologists, cardiologists and rehabilitation experts met with two dozen MS patients, assessed each one's physical capability, tailored exercises to it and offered training in motivation and self-image. Jimmie has plans to reach MS chapters throughout the country with this conditioning program, sponsored by the Jimmie Heuga Center, a $60,000-a-year nonprofit operation supported by gifts and benefits.

"Jimmie is changing medical thinking," says Labe Scheinberg, chairman of the medical advisory board to the National Multiple Sclerosis Society. "Many of us now tell our patients, 'You can't hurt yourself exercising. When you get tired, just stop.' Lots of doctors still wrap their patients in cotton wool, but reasonable exercise is definitely a trend. What Jimmie is saying is: Maximize your health. Get active. Get interested. There's nothing scientific about it. It's purely inspirational. But it works!"

That Jimmie Heuga's message is getting through is made clear by the thousands of letters he receives from people with MS who have heard him speak, seen him on television or read about him.

Still a Champion. That Jimmie Heuga's message is getting through is made clear by the thousands of letters he receives from people with MS who have heard him speak, seen him on television or read about him. A California woman confessed that she had been consumed by self-pity until she saw Jimmie on "CBS's Sports Sunday." "It changed my life," she wrote. "I feel a hundred percent better. I broke my foot doing the

bunny hop, then two weeks later broke the cast clear off while climbing Mount Tam!"

Most eloquent of all was the 32-year-old wife of a Dallas real-estate developer, who wrote: "Through exercise, my physical condition has improved, and I can play the piano again. Without your courage in dealing with your situation and speaking publicly about it, I would not be so happy today."

Enclosed with the letter was a $1,500 donation. Equally appreciated by Jimmie was the woman's penned afterthought: "I had felt that only 'losers' get crazy diseases. But there you are — a champion before; twice a champion now."

ONE WOMAN'S RACE ACROSS ALASKA

by Susan Butcher

**It is the toughest race of all — 1,000 miles
by dog sled across a vast and frozen land.
Susan Butcher was determined to win.**

TEKLA lies beside the sled, too tired to go on. I
look down at my most experienced lead dog
and curse my luck.

A wrong turn in a heavy snowstorm the first day of
the race has taken me 20 miles out of my way. The four
precious hours lost in regaining the trail have put me far
behind the front-runners in the world's longest sled-dog
race — the 1,000-mile Iditarod — which crosses Alaska
from Anchorage to Nome. More important, I have lost
Tekla for the remainder of the course.

The grueling race, held annually since 1973, follows a
route blazed in the early 1900s between the gold-rush
towns of Iditarod and Nome and the ice-free port of
Seward. In past years the race has taken competitors 12
to 32 days to complete.

Nome Council Koyuk
Solomon
White Mountain   Elim
        Golovin
        Shaktoolik
Bering   Kaltag
  Sea
        Unalakleet

Anvik Grayling Ophir McGrath
       Shageluk   Nikolai
         Iditarod Takotna   Alaska Range
                                Rohn
                              Finger Lake
                    Rainy Pass Skwentna
                  Rabbit Lake
                    Susitna   Wasilla
                                 Eagle River
                                 Anchorage

I was born into a comfortable family life in Cambridge, Mass. During childhood summers at the Maine seashore, I spent every waking hour learning about the outdoors. Of many pets, my favorite was my dog.

As I grew older, I yearned for a life that would combine dogs and the outdoors. Deep inside I also had this feeling that there was a place where I could breathe more freely, where my own hard work would be the measure of my success and the source of my existence.

I came to Alaska in 1975, hoping to find my dream. Today, from my cabin door 140 miles northwest of Fairbanks and 4 miles from my nearest neighbor, I look at my sled-dog team and know my dream is as real as Mount McKinley far beyond. And as challenging as the Iditarod.

> *I came to Alaska in 1975, hoping to find my dream. Today ... I look at my sled-dog team and know my dream is as real as Mount McKinley far beyond.*

For three years I lived in the wilderness, building and training a team for my first Iditarod in 1978. I finished 19th, barely in the money. (Only the first 20 into Nome share in some $100,000 in cash prizes.) I came in ninth the next year, fifth in 1980 and '81. This is the '82 race, and I am prepared to win.

Preparations for each year's race, held in early March, begin as soon as the last one is over. Heavy training starts in early September, and before long my dogs and I are hitting the trail well before the sun peeks over a nearby ridge. Good racers must be able to trot at 12 miles an hour, lope at 18. Mine are Alaskan huskies, bred for stamina and for good feet that won't be cut by ice, or form snowballs between the pads. They average 50 pounds and have long legs and slim builds.

Each one of my 50 dogs, however, has a distinct personality. I race only 15, but more are always being trained to keep this number at full strength. Every evening, after training runs of up to 60 miles, I invite some of my team into the cabin for a treat and a discussion of the day's workout. Copilot voices her opinion with a howl when I commend her performance. The others thump their tails as their names are mentioned.

When it's time to check paws for injuries, Tekla and Daiquiri roll on their backs, feet in the air, begging for attention.

February has arrived, and I must put together 1,500 pounds of food and equipment to be stashed at 24 checkpoints along the course: 75 burlap sacks to be filled with meat and fish, booties to protect paws, extra batteries for the headlamp I will use along the trail.

Meat must be cut into chunks for easy feeding en route. Honey balls must be made of ground beef, honey, vegetable oil, and vitamin and mineral supplements. Sleds are fitted with new plastic runners, bolts, lashings, supply bags.

The dogs and I arrive in Anchorage to join an eventual field of 54 mushers and 796 dogs. We hear talk of an icy trail with dangerous turns. This only adds to my nervousness. Now there is just one more day before I am out on the trail alone with my dogs and the life I love.

We hear talk of an icy trail with dangerous turns. This only adds to my nervousness.

There is so little snow in Anchorage this year that our start has been moved 52 miles north to Settlers Bay. The teams will leave the starting line at three-minute intervals; I will start 26th.

My dogs are so eager to get going that it takes ten people to hold them as earlier starters move out. My friend Kathy Jones, who helped raise my expense money, tucks herself onto the sled. The rules require each musher to carry a passenger for the first eight miles in case of early trouble.

My countdown begins, and then we're off! On an icy hill a mile out, we go into a slide; we hit a downed tree and roll over. Kathy and I feel only a few aches and pains, but three of the team, clearly shaken, are running off pace. Even so, we're making good time. "Gee, Tekla!" I cry. She pulls to the right, and we pass two teams.

Soon Kathy leaves us, and I continue on alone. Miles peel away, and snow begins as darkness falls. One by one, I overtake 22 teams; only 3 are ahead of me now.

Cracker, Ruff and Screamer quit pulling and begin to limp. As much as it will slow me, I load them onto the sled to prevent further injury. They add 150 pounds for the remaining dogs to pull.

Mile after mile I ride behind them on the runners; I should have seen the Skwentna checkpoint by now. I sense something is wrong. At dawn a musher approaches from the opposite direction and hails me: "We're at least ten miles off course!"

I turn my team around. My misery cannot be expressed. All year I have nurtured but one thought: to win. Now—after a useless 20-mile detour—my hopes are dashed.

Tekla starts to limp. The strain of those extra miles without rest has been too much. I take her out of the lead and put Copilot up with Ali.

At 6:55 A.M. we straggle into Skwentna, a full four hours behind my schedule. Checking in at postmaster Joe Delia's cabin, my dogs and I are like robots. I feed them, and then take Cracker, Ruff and Screamer to a drop area where they can be flown home. I massage Tekla's shoulder. I can't afford to lose her this early in the race.

We push on. Forty-five miles farther, at Finger Lake, I know my limping Tekla has reached her limit. Tears roll down my cheeks. She, who led my team all the way in my first three Iditarods, who has saved my life more than once, who can even read my mind, now has to be left behind. Her sorrow seems as great as mine as she watches me from where she's tied under a tree to await the flight home.

With only 11 weary dogs left, I strike out again for Nome, still 938 miles away. After just ten miles, I know we have to stop. I lie in the snow next to Ali and Copilot. They cuddle up against me, and I massage their shoulders and legs. Other teams flash past. My resolve is shaken, but I'm not ready to give up.

On the move again, I think only of reaching the Rohn checkpoint, where I will spend a compulsory 24-hour layover. In these first two days on the trail, I have had only four hours' sleep.

As we climb into Rainy Pass, my mind is not fully

focused. I let go of the sled so the team can clamber up the steep bank unencumbered by my weight. But I have badly misjudged the energy of my dogs; soon they are out of sight.

For six miles I pursue them. Around one more bend and there they are, the sled on its side but intact. They bark and wag their tails as if to say, "Where have *you* been?" We arrive at Rohn at 5:01 P.M., now two days out of Settlers Bay.

After the 24-hour rest and four hot meals, my team is yowling and barking to be off, and my determination to stay in the race is firmer than ever. Even Jimmy is running hard, despite sore feet that I have been treating with medication.

The falling snow grows heavier, wiping out the trail, but I keep going. I catch up with the leaders, who have lost their way and are waiting for daylight.

To this point it has been every musher for himself. But now we must work together, taking turns at trail-breaking through the deep snow. As soon as possible, we'll be off again on our own.

> *I let go of the sled so the team can clamber up the steep bank unencumbered by my weight. But I have badly misjudged the energy of my dogs; soon they are out of sight.*

We travel in this tedious and time-consuming manner for 4½ days and 353 miles. Skies are clear, but temperatures drop to 45 degrees below zero as I start out alone down the frozen Yukon River. If I stay too long on the sled, I risk serious frostbite. Too long jogging behind can impair my lungs. So I alternate between running and riding. Jimmy's feet are worse; I'm forced to drop him at Galena.

A raging storm moves in, burying the trail. Those of us in the lead bunch up again to break trail. But after 50 miles we must take refuge in a trapper's tent for the night.

Another day's travel brings us to Unalakleet. Only 271 miles to Nome! The weather worsens; winds rise to 60 miles an hour. Visibility drops to near zero. My eyelashes and the dogs' freeze shut, and I stop often to clear their eyes and check their feet.

It is midnight. Even with my headlamp I cannot see the driftwood tripods that mark the trail across these miles of flat, featureless country. Groping from tripod to tripod, I finally reach Shaktoolik with a frostbitten face. Lucy Sockpealuk welcomes us to her home. Even the dogs. It is too cold outside for them to rest easy, and the wind blows away their pans.

By morning, winds are gusting up to 80 MPH, piling up 30-foot drifts. I wait 52 hours in the village before the storm lets up. All the mushers there resume the race with new strength and spirit. Only 231 miles to go, but all of them tough. We push through the continuing storm to White Mountain, seven lead teams traveling close together.

Taboo, worn out from punching too long through heavy snow, must drop out, leaving me with just 9 dogs. Emmitt Peters is now running 10, Rick Swenson, 12, and Jerry Austin, 14. Even so, I feel this is still a wide-open race.

Forty miles from the finish we run into strong winds again. By the time the storm has died away, Ali, my best command leader, is tired of taking orders. So I put Stripe up front with Copilot. Both dogs drive hard; the team picks up its pace.

Soon I am in fifth place, only a short distance behind Rick, Jerry, Emmitt, and Ernie Baumgartner. The final push is on: 30 miles to go. My adrenalin is pumping.

I pass Ernie and pull away. I pass Emmitt, but he stays right on my tail. Through the last checkpoint we dash; only 22 miles now. Someone yells out that Rick and Jerry are just two minutes ahead of me. Emmitt remains close behind.

Stripe falters. I need Ali up there. Is he rested enough? I have to take the chance. The change is quick — 40 seconds — but Emmitt is halfway by me when I holler at Ali and Copilot, "Go! Go! Go!" The instant I feel my dogs diving forward, I know I have done the trick. I soon outdistance Emmitt.

Ali has raced with me to Nome before and senses he's into the homestretch. He knows his job and gives it his all. The other dogs respond to his leadership. I chase hard and pass Jerry. But there's still Rick, barely visible in the distance.

My dogs and I try with all our might to overtake him, but he still beats us into Nome by 3 minutes and 43 seconds. The race has lasted 16 days. Cheers ring out around me. I gratefully accept a second-place prize of $16,000. The last musher will not cross the finish line until ten days later.

> *The wilderness is my life now, and the Iditarod its ultimate experience.*

The wilderness is my life now, and the Iditarod its ultimate experience. I love Alaska and the opportunity it has given me to realize my dreams. I have only one dream to go: to be No. 1.

Susan Butcher went on to win four Iditarod competitions — in 1986, 1987, 1988 and 1990 — tying the record of four Iditarod victories held by Rick Swenson. Her record finishes in 1986, 1987 and 1990 established her as the best long-distance musher in the world. In 1990 she also won Minnesota's 500-mile John Beargrease Sled Dog Marathon in record time. She retired after completing the 1994 Iditarod, in order to be able to spend more time with her lawyer-musher husband Dave Monson, whom she married in 1985. Although she did not compete, Susan trained dogs for the 1995 Iditarod and worked as a commentator at the starting line, while seven months pregnant.

MEL BLOUNT: RESCUER OF LOST BOYS

by Mark Roman

He once battled in Super Bowls.
Now he fights to save young lives.

MEL BLOUNT easily remembers the hard times growing up on a Georgia dirt farm. He went barefoot, and the family home was without plumbing or electricity.

But poverty, his father always said, was no excuse for failure. "You may resent the way I push you," James Blount would tell his 11 children, "but hard work is the only way not to be poor all your lives."

Almost as soon as they could walk, all the Blount kids had chores. His first job, recalls Mel, the youngest of seven boys, was stacking tobacco on a wagon in the golden light of a kerosene lantern. "Every morning. Early. Before the dew dries," his father ordered. If Mel lingered in bed, his father would overturn the mattress, point a finger and say, "There's work to be done."

The boy discovered there was a pleasure in stacking more and more tobacco, setting goals for himself and surpassing them. But his biggest reward was the simple praise he heard from his father: "Fine job, son. Fine job."

Sundays, before church, the Blounts would kneel on the living-room floor as Mel's father led the family in prayer. Good will always prevail in the face of evil, and God helps those who help themselves, he'd remind his family. Even as a boy, Mel knew that hard work, pride and responsibility were values to live by.

One summer morning a pack of baying hounds had bounded over the fence of the Blounts' small Vidalia farm. Right behind appeared an angry group of armed white men, led by the local sheriff, looking for a distant relative of the family.

Mel's mother pleaded to no avail for her husband to stay inside. As the tall black farmer strode toward the intruders, one by one they lowered their guns and stepped aside. "My family obeys the law," he told the sheriff. "You'll find no criminals in THIS house! Now get your men off my land."

He had not yet been born, but Mel would hear that story of courage time and again as he grew up. Later he would draw upon it for strength as he would on the other lessons his father taught.

After church on Sundays, Mel's older brothers played "country football." The boys hit hard—and the kid brother was a natural. The head football coach of Southern University at Baton Rouge, La., heard about "this skinny kid from Georgia who runs like hell" and offered the high-school senior a scholarship.

Mel couldn't quell his anxiety when he first saw the university's campus and the well-dressed students. *I grew up barefoot*, he thought. *How will I survive here?* But his father's parting words rang in his ear: "Mel, trust your upbringing. It will always help you make the right choices."

> *One summer morning a pack of baying hounds had bounded over the fence of the Blounts' small Vidalia farm. Right behind appeared an angry group of armed white men, led by the local sheriff.*

He followed his father's advice and stuck to his dirt-farm ways. He arose at dawn every day to work out, and he studied long and hard. When classwork or practice tried his endurance, Mel would hear his father's voice: "Son, there's work to be done," and he would grit his teeth and try harder.

One day Mel received a phone call from his mother. "Your father's dead," she wept. "He had a heart attack." The ride home seemed endless. *I just wish he could have seen me play,* Mel kept saying to himself. His regret became even greater when in his senior year he was named All-American.

In 1970 Mel was selected in the National Football League draft by the Pittsburgh Steelers, perhaps the weakest team in the NFL. *That's okay,* he thought. *I'll just get plenty of chances to prove myself.*

During the next 14 years Mel Blount became a key in Pittsburgh's vaunted defense. His aggressive play made

Mel Blount
with some of the boys who have come to live at his youth home

him a household name among fans as he helped lead the team to four Super Bowl victories.

Then, after one particularly tough contest, the cornerback sat quietly by his locker. After thousands of grueling tackles he had begun to grow weary of the game. A remark Steeler coach Chuck Noll had made in a locker-room speech rang in his ears: "Football isn't everything. What will be your life's work?"

That question burned inside Mel Blount for months. He was to discover the answer he searched for during one of his visits to the Georgia farm where he grew up and where his young fans would drop by whenever he returned.

"My parents leave me by myself all the time," one admiring youngster confided. "I just dropped out of school," confessed another. Mel's brother Clinton pulled him aside. "There are boys like these all over the country," he said. "They could use your help."

At that moment, Mel Blount, football superstar, realized he had discovered his life's mission: *I'll build these boys a dirt farm of their own,* he thought. They would learn the lessons and values his father had taught him.

In 1983, his last year in pro football, Mel and his brother opened a licensed youth home 200 feet from his mother's back door. Mel put thousands of dollars of his own money into the project and raised thousands more with help from former teammates and business contacts.

A judge in Fort Lauderdale, Fla., who heard of the project, was among the first to call. "I have a boy who's been stealing," he told Mel. "He's got an attitude problem." *Exactly the kind of boy I want,* Mel thought.

One week later, a security van pulled onto the Blount farm, and a 16-year-old boy climbed out. Malnourished and jittery from beatings by his stepfather, the youngster affected street-tough ways. But when Mel shook his hand, he learned his first lesson. "Son," said Mel, "always shake hands firmly. Look people straight in the eye, tell them your name and say, 'Pleased to meet you.'" Despite himself, the boy answered, "Yessir!"

Juvenile-delinquency agencies began sending other neglected and abused kids, many with criminal records.

Officials viewed Mel's dirt farm as a last alternative to sentencing.

Its routine came straight from Blount's childhood: up at dawn to clean the stables; off to the local public school; after classes, supervised study; then more farm chores; and, finally, early lights out. The boys washed and ironed their own clothes and did the pots, pans and dishes after every meal. Rooms had to be spotless. Mel and Clinton inspected every closet and drawer.

When the boys performed well, they earned trips to a local steakhouse or a shopping center. But any boy who slacked off had to stay home. If he repeatedly misbehaved, he was sent, shovel in hand, to dig up one of the farm's tree stumps. "Stumping can take all day," moaned one boy. "It gives you a lot of time to think about what you did."

Soon, parents were calling Mel Blount a "miracle worker." Of his more than 100 "graduates," about 85 percent had remained in school, got jobs and led clean lives.

Each day the Pittsburgh papers reported shootings, stabbings and beatings in the inner city. Mel believed he could save young boys from this savage world of crime.

In 1989, Mel bought another farm near Taylorstown, 40 miles from Pittsburgh. Each day the Pittsburgh papers reported shootings, stabbings and beatings in the inner city. Mel believed he could save young boys from this savage world of crime.

The farm had a 200-year-old house, and all he needed to begin operations was a permit from the township. But Mel Blount had not anticipated the furor his request would bring.

At first, ugly warnings appeared in mailboxes in Taylorstown. "These ghetto monkeys will bring your people nothing but trouble!" During the following weeks, a boisterous "concerned citizens" group lobbied local parents, and the racist fliers kept coming. A township supervisor was heard to say, "It's very possible that this could be a great program, but it's also very possible that it could be a great harm to the community."

On August 4, 1989, the day before Mel Blount's induction into the Pro Football Hall of Fame, two youths drove up the driveway of the Blount home and fired shots from a .44 Magnum. The next day, in his Hall of Fame speech, Mel spoke proudly of giving troubled kids a "second chance." He revealed the racial problems he was facing, and his message was strong: "The Mel Blount Youth Home is going up. We will make it work."

One month later, hundreds of people filled the local high-school auditorium for the hearing to debate the home's operating permit. Throughout often angry opposition, Mel Blount sat stoic and silent.

> ... hundreds of people filled the local high-school auditorium for the hearing ...Throughout often angry opposition, Mel Blount sat stoic and silent.

Then a minister rose to his feet and declared his support for Mel's request. Next a businessman spoke in its favor. Then a homemaker. Mel felt a surge of pride and gratitude as the people of the township made themselves heard. Within weeks, the supervisors gave Blount the go-ahead.

Three weeks after the good news came an event Mel Blount says he will always remember. A racist mob began gathering near the farm. *What would my father do?* Mel asked himself. Just as his father had done with the sheriff and his men, Mel had to confront the bigots.

When he drove up to the demonstrators, the men glanced at Mel's familiar face and looked quickly away. None of them had the courage to say anything. Then Mel noticed a boy in a robe inching closer.

He's no older than my kids at home, Mel thought sadly. "Son," he asked, "can I see one of those fliers you're holding?" Mel read the ugly words and looked into the boy's dark eyes. The youth averted his gaze, apparently embarrassed in the presence of Mel's courage.

On Christmas morning 1990 at the Pennsylvania home, Mel Blount called all his youngsters to the living room. As they entered, they gasped in surprise. Under the tree were piles of beautifully wrapped gifts.

"They're from the people of this town," Blount said. "Christmas is the season of giving, and these folks are praying for you and wish the best for you."

A few days earlier, the boys had presented a gift to Mel. It was a handmade booklet they had worked on in secret for weeks. It described the Youth Home, and on the cover the youngsters had drawn a picture of a boy reaching for a distant star. Mel could not remember receiving a more precious present.

He is not a genius, Mel Blount says. Nor a social worker with fancy theories. He's just a simple country boy with the hope of saving lost youngsters. "You have to guide boys, lead them in the proper direction, teach them discipline, or they'll be wild their whole lives," he says. And in his ear he hears a voice, the voice of his father: *If you work harder, you can do even better.*

SKATING TO THE TOP

by Susan Jacoby

They're the best!
How do they make it look so easy?

BRIAN BOITANO is spending his usual "day at the office." It is March 1995, and he is at a dingy ice rink in Berkeley, Calif. Approaching his 32nd birthday, the slender five-foot-eleven-inch skater with a receding hairline is doing what he has done nearly every day since he was eight — practicing his jumps and spins — five, ten, 50 times. Olympic gold medalist in 1988 and current world professional champion, Boitano holds time and the pain of a damaged knee at bay to perform at a level once considered unthinkable for someone his age.

At the same time, in suburban Detroit, 13-year-old Erin Sutton, a brown-eyed blonde who stands five-foot-two, is living out the early part of the Olympic dream. Erin is not a star — yet — but she has just taken a huge step toward international competition by winning the 1995 U.S. Novice Ladies' Championship. A resilient seventh-grader, she puts in two hours of practice before school each day. No one has to push Erin: her dream provides all the push she needs.

Each winter's competitive figure-skating season really begins during the prior spring in the indoor ice world where practice begins before sunrise. Whether the skater is a veteran or a novice, it takes months of work to produce the three to five minutes of heart-stopping leaps, dizzying spins and intricate footwork that keep fans on the edge of their seats.

Figure skating is unquestionably the breakthrough sport of the '90s, drawing sellout crowds for live performances and earning television ratings previously reserved for professional baseball and basketball.

Skating's popularity, which skyrocketed after the 1994 Olympic confrontation between Tonya Harding and Nancy Kerrigan, is turning the formerly elite pastime into a sport with mass appeal and millions in annual earnings for star performers.

Brian Boitano and Erin Sutton share a fierce dedication to their sport. And while they have had many experiences in common, the two have very different perspectives on figure skating.

The Dream. When Brian was eight, his parents took him to see an ice show during Christmas vacation. Transfixed, he begged to have skating lessons at a rink near their home in Sunnyvale, Calif. At his first group lesson, Brian, trying to master a basic spin, was able to whirl three times faster than the other children. The children's coach, Linda Leaver, who still coaches Boitano, moved him to her more advanced class.

Only a few weeks later, Brian mastered five different single-revolution jumps in one lesson — jumps that take most skaters at least several months to perfect. "I went home and told my husband, 'That little boy is going to be a world champion,'" Leaver recalls.

Erin was four years old when she begged her parents to let her try out the ice rink at a shopping mall near their home. Since then, she has displayed the same kind of determination that Boitano did 24 years ago.

At 6:30 one Saturday morning last April, Erin was already practicing at an ice rink in Plymouth, Mich. "Skating is the most important thing to me," she says. "It is hard work, but it's so much fun." To warm up, she jumped rope off-ice with her girlfriends, then did stretching exercises.

At the U.S. National Championships, there are three competitive levels leading up to the Olympics: novice (which Erin won earlier this year); junior (in which she'll

> *Brian mastered five different single-revolution jumps in one lesson — jumps that take most skaters at least several months to perfect.*

be competing at the 1996 national championships); and senior, the top level, which feeds into the Olympics. Erin's current goal is to make the 1998 Olympic team.

The Challenge. The blade of a figure skate measures ¾ inch wide and is ground slightly concave so that one or the other of the two edges grips the ice while the skate glides on a thin film of water. (The water is produced by the pressure of the skate melting the ice.) Every jump or spin begins on the inside or outside edge, which digs into the ice and, along with the toe pick on some jumps, helps provide traction for takeoff.

At top competitive levels, skaters routinely take off on one edge, revolve three times in the air and land on one foot — always moving backward on the outside edge of the blade. Tilt too far to the outside or inside on takeoff, and you either won't get off the ground or your body won't be in the proper upright position in the air. You're likely to fall — or, at the very least, put down a hand or the other foot to steady yourself — and destroy your competitive chances. It takes years of practice before a skater can progress from single- and double-revolution jumps to triple jumps and land them with any degree of reliability. "The goal is to make it look easy," says Boitano. And that's exactly what he does: Boitano has fallen in competition only twice.

While no competitive skater has ever been killed in a fall, the fear of falling can kill a career.

While no competitive skater has ever been killed in a fall, the fear of falling can kill a career. The most successful skaters are those who've mastered the fear.

Boitano has — but now, as an older skater, his main concern is maintaining his body. Groin pulls, torn ligaments, sprains, a broken arm or leg are part of every career. But after a certain age, athletes develop arthritis and torn cartilage in the joints that receive the heaviest use — in Brian's case there are torn tendons in his right knee. "How many times have I landed on my right leg?"

he asks with a grin. "Maybe 400,000? I don't even want to think about it."

Doctors have told Boitano that even new arthroscopic surgery techniques won't repair his knee. So, besides three hours of skating practice, Boitano's daily training regimen includes whirlpool baths, deep tissue massage and sessions on an exercise bike. Strengthening the muscles that protect his joints is the best remedy for his problem.

Aging and chronic pain are unimaginable to Erin Sutton. After the warm-up exercises, she began working on her triple-loop jump with her coaches Theresa McKendry and Gerry Williams. The loop is particularly difficult because a skater must take off backward on one foot using the outside blade edge — without any help from the pointed toe picks at the front of the blade.

"Erin doesn't give up," McKendry says. "There's nothing a coach can do to give a child that attitude. She either has it or she doesn't."

Traveling back on her right foot, Erin leaned on the outside edge of her blade, pulled in her arms and her left foot, sprang into the air and attempted to stay up long enough to whirl around three times. Not quite able to complete the three revolutions, she landed off-balance five, ten, 20, up to 30 times over the course of two daily lessons, ending the jump sprawled on her backside, shaking ice shavings out of her ponytail. Each time, she popped back up for another try. "Erin doesn't give up," McKendry says. "There's nothing a coach can do to give a child that attitude. She either has it or she doesn't."

The Limit. Boitano has a style that can only be described as classic. Where some men wear garish costumes or engage in bare-chested machismo, he invariably glides onto the ice in a simple costume, performs to a wide range of music, including classical and popular, and lets his skating speak for itself. In response to audience ovations, he often conveys his appreciation by bowing, hand on heart. He is an unapologetic skating purist.

In competitions, Boitano does more than he needs to do to win. At last year's pro championships, for example, he was the only competitor to complete a triple-triple combination, in which the skater propels himself into a second triple jump immediately after landing the first. Boitano explains: "The satisfaction is in knowing you've pushed this sport, this art, to the limit."

Erin also believes in pushing herself to the limit. At last year's national novice championships, she landed a fiendishly difficult move called the Tano lutz — named after Boitano, its inventor. On all jump takeoffs, skaters normally whip both arms in close to the body to help accomplish their revolutions in the air. The Tano double or triple, by contrast, is performed with one arm held aloft, a variation that incurs more air resistance, thus requiring greater leg strength for the takeoff.

Whether double or triple, it's a move few skaters have attempted — the equivalent of a baseball pitcher's delivering a fast ball with one arm tied behind his back. "I just thought it would be fun to do," Erin said afterward.

Before meets, Erin meticulously makes a list of the jumps in her routine and later gives herself a check mark for each clean landing. Recently she added reminders of fine points — such as smiling at the audience.

The Cost. Serious skaters — and their families — don't lead ordinary lives.

Boitano, youngest of four children of a well-to-do bank president, attended public high school but spent as much time on the ice as he did in school. Every day, he skated from 5 A.M. to 10 A.M. before starting classes. "You can't be focused on the Olympics and have the usual teen-age life," Boitano says. "In the summer when everyone else was tan, I was pale."

Fortunately for Brian, his parents, Lew and Donna, didn't pressure him.

"They did this for me because I loved to skate, not because they thought I could get rich from it," he says. "They made lots of sacrifices for me but always said, 'You

can quit any time you want.' That freedom is the greatest gift anyone could give a child."

Regardless of whether Erin becomes a world champion, her parents, airline pilot Ken Sutton and his wife, Kay, are determined to do everything they can to help her pursue her goal. "I suppose a lot of parents have dreams of glory," says Kay, "but we'd like to see her skate a while longer for the pure joy of it."

Last September, when Erin entered eighth grade, her mother began tutoring her at home. The Suttons were concerned about the physical toll of a "workday" that began at 5:30 A.M. Now Erin is able to sleep on a more normal schedule and practice in the afternoon. Next year the Suttons hope to find a high school with flexible scheduling so their daughter can attend regular classes.

One reality the Suttons are facing is the staggering cost of training, which for a serious skater can easily reach $50,000 a year. Erin takes 15 private lessons a week at approximately $50 for each 45-minute session. Her custom-made skates cost $750 a pair, and she requires at least two pairs each year. Then there is the cost of costumes and travel to competitions.

For this reason, the financial payoff for figure skaters remains both an incentive and a reward. At major competitions during the pro season, prizes range from $40,000 to $200,000, depending on where a performer places. Some annual exhibitions, such as the Tom Collins Tour of World Figure Skating Champions, pay appearance fees of more than $750,000 for headliners. Add TV specials and product endorsements, and a star like Boitano may make several million dollars a year.

The Competition. Olympic competition is divided into two stages: a "short" program, with strictly required moves, and a "long" program, which gives skaters more freedom to choreograph their moves. The short program counts 30 percent and the long, 70. A perfect score is 6.0. In the short program, specified tenths of a point must be deducted for a fall and for other mistakes,

such as a two-footed landing or the omission of a required move.

Such deductions are huge in a competition where world standings may be decided by one-tenth of a point. In the long program, the negative effect of a fall may be offset by the artistry and technical difficulty of the overall performance.

Boitano entered the 1994 Olympics with a shot at becoming the first American since Dick Button to win a second gold medal. (Button won in 1948 and 1952.) That evening in Lillehammer, Norway, Boitano began the short program with a perfectly executed Tano triple lutz. His next move was a 3½ revolution triple axel — the most difficult triple jump in the sport.

While he was aloft, all looked textbook-perfect. But then — for only the second time in his competitive career — he fell. Knowledgeable spectators gasped, knowing the five-tenths deduction had probably ruined Boitano's chance at a gold medal. To this day, neither Boitano nor his coach knows what he did to cause the fall. "That's skating," Boitano says. "You can be off-balance just a tiny fraction, and there goes the landing."

Boitano fought back to complete the rest of his short program flawlessly, and today he reflects: "I look at the experience as a gift — just to have performed in the Olympics at an age when skaters used to retire."

For a skater Erin's age, a fall in competition is not devastating, but rather an opportunity to learn. Last July she was the youngest participant in the ladies' event at the U.S. Olympic Festival, a showcase for young, aspiring Olympians. Skating before TV cameras for the first time, she began her routine with the same concentration she had displayed in practice. But while preparing for her entry into a triple loop, she seemed to be slightly off-balance and fell on the landing.

> *To this day, neither Boitano nor his coach knows what he did to cause the fall. "That's skating," Boitano says. "You can be off-balance just a tiny fraction, and there goes the landing."*

She took the fall like a veteran, jumping up and continuing with her routine. A few seconds later, she landed a perfect triple toe/double toe jump combination. Overall, Erin performed both the short and long programs more consistently than her competitors — and she won the event.

The Thrill. Brian Boitano's work habits are legendary. On this day, he is at the Berkeley rink, focusing on a new routine he has choreographed, a series of tricky steps called "footwork." The routine demands that he place his ankles, knees and hips in a wide variety of positions, turning his joints inward or outward at 45-degree angles.

After an hour of practice, Boitano suddenly shifts into one of his signature moves — a spin appropriately named the "death drop." Using his left foot for a whirling take-off, he leaps high into the air and comes down on the other foot in a sitting position. Unless you already know what to expect, this looks like a fall — until you see that he's spinning, seated, with perfect control. Boitano smiles exultantly: The move has turned out exactly as planned.

Boitano checks his watch and realizes he is late for his date with the exercise bike. He squints at the bright sunlight as he walks out of Berkeley Iceland. After nearly a quarter-century of skating, Brian Boitano still has no California tan.

HEART OF
AN IRONMAN

by John G. Hubbell

**Sometimes, being a champion is
simply knowing when not to quit.**

I N 1983, GEORGE YATES was a world-class triathlete. The previous season, he had finished seventh in
Hawaii's grueling Ironman Triathlon, one of the most
punishing tests of endurance ever devised. He swam 2.4
miles in the ocean, then bicycled 112 miles, and finally ran
a 26.2-mile marathon — all through rugged conditions
and all in just over ten hours. That same year, he came in
sixth in Florida's Gulf Coast Triathlon and eighth in the
World Championship in Nice, France. Overall, the 28-
year-old was the world's ninth-ranked triathlete, and he
was training relentlessly to make himself No. 1.

Yates worked part-time in a bicycle shop, giving him
the freedom to travel to competitions and pursue his
goal. Now back home, in Corona del Mar, Calif., preparing for the Ironman Triathlon, Yates began awakening with

a stiff back. Increasing knee pain forced him to run and bike gingerly. He shrugged off each symptom as the result of his continuous training.

But from the outset of the Ironman Triathlon that fall, Yates felt as if he were competing in slow motion. He struggled mightily, only to finish 48th. *What in the world is wrong with me?* he wondered.

> Yates felt as if he were competing in slow motion. . . . What in the world is wrong with me? he wondered.

Prisoner in a Body. Over the next few months, the symptoms worsened. On the morning of April 17, 1984, Yates was unable to get out of bed, his whole body racked by excruciating pain. For five days he lay helpless, tended by friends, as his knees ballooned to the size of grapefruits and his once-powerful muscles visibly weakened. He was frantic. "Stay in bed and get lots of rest until this virus runs its course," a doctor told him.

One morning, with no help at hand, he tried to reach the bathroom. An hour later, a friend found him sprawled unconscious on the floor. Yates could not move, and so exquisite was the pain that he could not bear to be touched. It took paramedics more than an hour to move him into an ambulance.

During two weeks of testing at Newport Beach's Hoag Memorial Hospital, Yates's condition deteriorated. Pain medications were ineffective; his weight plummeted from 165 to 125 pounds. Finally doctors diagnosed the condition as acute ankylosing spondylitis, a spinal arthritis for which there is no cure. Remission was possible, but his case was so severe that residual joint damage was likely. He would need a walker or possibly a wheelchair to get around, the doctor said.

Yates couldn't believe what he was hearing. Was the body that had so recently accomplished extraordinary feats now to become his prison? "There must be *something* that can be done — I'm not just going to throw in the towel!" But the doctor shook his head sadly. Mary and George Yates took their son home to their house in Glendale, Calif.

A Distant Goal. A few days later, Yates's parents wheeled him into the examining room of Dr. John Curd, a rheumatologist at La Jolla's Scripps Research Clinic. The doctor was immediately concerned. He had seen many young people sick with debilitating arthritis, but rarely a case as acute as this one. Yates could barely move; the only spark of life came from his eyes, which glowed with a determined intensity.

Dr. Curd hospitalized him for further tests, determining that Yates had either ankylosing spondylitis or Reiter's Syndrome, a similar form of arthritis. Even with a possible remission, victims of such a severe attack rarely resume any intense athletic pursuits. Curd wondered how a world-class athlete would react to this grim prognosis. He soon found out.

"I'm going to compete again — in the Ironman," Yates declared.

"I'll do all I can to help," Curd responded, "but I can only take you so far." If Yates was to achieve his goal, it would be 99 percent up to him.

"That's what I wanted to hear, doctor," Yates said. "Let's get on with it!"

The first challenge was to sit up in bed. Curd treated the swollen joints with heat; it didn't help. Neither did cold. He put Yates on the largest possible doses of an anti-inflammatory agent.

After ten days, Yates was able to sit up, and a few days later he was in physical therapy, engaged in an immensely frustrating effort to make his legs move.

Within a month, Yates could manage a walker competently. Now that he had some mobility, Dr. Curd discharged him with instructions to take his medications and check in frequently.

Making Something Happen. A few weeks later, Yates, using the walker, presented himself to Dr. Kenneth Forsythe, a sports-medicine specialist in Santa Monica. "I want to come all the way back," Yates told the doctor. "I am going to give it everything I have."

"What do you ultimately want to accomplish?"

"To place top ten in the Ironman."

Dr. Forsythe looked thoughtful. In his experience, highly motivated people had achieved remarkable things. But like the other doctors, he questioned whether Yates could again become a serious contender in the Ironman. "Okay," Forsythe finally said. "You've got the desire, so I'll help you all I can."

The doctor designed a program that had Yates swimming, lifting weights and working out on an electronic bicycle and rowing machine up to four hours per day, five days a week. Activities that would stretch muscles excessively, put too much strain on the joints or increase pain were avoided.

The pain, however, was constant. Even sitting still brought no relief. But Yates willed the pain from his mind. He was going to get better and compete again, or die trying. Progress was slow, almost imperceptible. "He was at it, every day," the doctor recalls. "Just sort of creeping along like a tortoise, trying to make something happen."

Often when Yates awakened in the morning, he hurt so much he had to argue with himself to crawl out of bed. But his competitive experience had taught him that the key to success is an unbreakable mental discipline. He dared not set goals and then fail to try to reach them. Sometimes when he returned home from workouts, he looked so haggard that his mother would cry. Friends urged him to take it easy. But Yates would never turn away from the greatest challenge of his life.

Spur to Success. When he started training under Dr. Forsythe in early July, his first goal was to walk unassisted by the end of August. Around this time, Dr. Curd put Yates on a different arthritis drug, Azulfidine. In less than a week, this brought a partial remission; the swelling in Yates's knees and ankles stopped. But the drug could not restore his atrophied muscles and damaged joints. Yates kept pushing, however, and on August 17, still in great pain, he walked alone for the first time in four months.

To achieve his other goals, Yates surrounded himself with friends who never stopped trying to reach their

own full potential and thus were a constant spur to excellence. He called on one of them, Michael Shermer, for help with his next target: to be back on a bicycle by the end of November. Besides being a world-class marathon cyclist, Shermer was an associate professor of psychology. He had not seen Yates for some time and was flabbergasted when they met at the biking course outside Pasadena's Rose Bowl. He recalls: "Here was this superb athlete who now had to lift his legs one at a time out of a car, then pull himself upright and shuffle along."

Shermer had to raise Yates onto his bike that first day. Cycling was out of the question; coasting was an achievement. But within a week, Yates was able to pedal a short distance. After six weeks he pedaled an entire lap — 3.1 miles. The pain in his legs was agonizing, and he was exhausted.

"But you *did* it, George," said Shermer triumphantly. "You're making it happen!"

Next time I'll do two laps, Yates promised himself. But the following day, after one lap, he hurt just as much. Enough was enough, he announced.

"You can do it, and you've got to do it!" Shermer insisted. This badgering was precisely why Yates had enlisted Shermer's help, and it worked. Yates pedaled a second lap. Within a few weeks, he doubled that to four laps, then on to eight.

> One morning in early March, 1985, Yates realized he had "sort of jogged" up a couple of flights of stairs at the clinic. *I'm getting there,* he told himself. *I'm getting close.*

"Getting Close." At one of Yates's monthly checkups at Scripps, Dr. Curd remarked, "George, you're amazing! Whatever you're doing, keep doing it."

By now, one thing he was not doing was taking his pain medication on a daily basis, as prescribed. It induced lethargy, so he cut the dosage to three days per week, deciding he could live with a certain amount of pain.

One morning in early March 1985, Yates realized he had "sort of jogged" up a couple of flights of stairs at the clinic. *I'm getting there,* he told himself. *I'm getting close.*

By the end of the month, he was out jogging for real, and could bicycle up to 30 miles at a time. There was always pain, but it was now overshadowed by a growing sense of accomplishment.

By May he felt ready to compete, and Dr. Forsythe agreed he could try a triathlon being held in Los Angeles in June. It involved a 0.6-mile swim, a 24.8-mile bike race and a 6.2-mile run. Out of some 400 contestants, Yates finished 48th! Even he could hardly believe what he had done.

He now focused on the 1985 Ironman, only four months away, pushing his training to the limit. He needed hundreds of ice bags to soothe joints that often seemed on fire. But he had determined that nothing would stop him.

More than 1,000 contestants dived into the sea for the 2.4-mile swim off the island of Hawaii. Yates was 79th out of the water, to begin on the bicycle segment: 112 miles across rugged terrain. Other competitors, old friends, were nervous: "George, take it easy. Are you okay?"

"Don't worry," he kept replying. "Just let me do what I'm doing." By the end of the bike race he had overtaken 73 racers and was in sixth place!

Proud Moment. Yates stayed in the top 20 through mile after mile of the marathon. At the 20-mile aid station, he had to stop and rest; only six miles to go — but his legs stiffened and his knees locked. A doctor massaged the legs. But when Yates tried to run, he almost fell on his face.

"There's no way I'm not finishing this thing!" he told the doctor. Full of pain, he walked stiff-legged, as fast as he could. In those final miles 115 people passed him. He was heartbroken; but at the same time, thinking of all he had been through in the past 16 months, he enjoyed the proudest moment of his life when he crossed the finish line, placing 134th.

George Yates has been competing ever since. In the 1986 Ironman, he had to walk the entire marathon, finishing 911th in a field of 1,039. In 1987, he placed 193rd out of 1,381. This past year, he finished 330th out of 1,275. Only ten people have competed more often than he in this most prestigious of triathlons.

Yates might not be the athlete he once was but he is a far more rounded competitor. "I used to be focused inwardly," he says, "on my own accomplishments. Not anymore."

Recently named to the Board of Governors for the Southern California chapter of the Arthritis Foundation, he has set a new goal for himself — to get his message across to the more than 37 million arthritis victims in this country. "I want all of them to know they don't have to accept this disease passively — that they should take their problems by the scruff of the neck and deal with them. The way to make positive things happen is to find the right help, set realistic goals and do what it takes to meet them. Don't let anything ruin the only life you have to live."

MEET THE FORMIDABLE MICHEL VAUTROT

by Gérard Ejnes

The world's best soccer referee faces his toughest match.

O N WEDNESDAY, October 11, 1989, Michel Vautrot landed in Bogotá, Colombia, to referee what the International Soccer Federation called a "high-risk match." Colombia was to host the Israeli team in a qualifying round for the 1990 World Cup. Because enormous interests were at stake, there was a good chance the match would be marred by disturbances both on the field and in the stands.

In Colombia the Medellín Drug Cartel controls clandestine soccer betting, and, for them, putting the squeeze on a referee is standard procedure. The drug barons have even claimed credit for the murder of a Colombian referee, accusing him of having caused the Medellín team to lose a game. But this situation did not stop Vautrot. "I know there is a drug war going on in this country," he told the press upon arrival. "I have been told that the drug lords try to control soccer. But I'm not frightened."

Throughout the 90-minute match on the following Sunday, Vautrot followed the play closely, running alongside the 22 players, catching every misplay without making a single mistake. To the inevitable protests, he calmly mimed the reasons for his decisions, making sure the teams understood them clearly. Colombia won a hard-fought match, 1–0. And there was no violence in the Metropolitan Stadium of Barranquilla.

The Federation's choice of sending Vautrot to Bogotá was deliberate. Named the world's best soccer referee in both 1988 and 1989, France's Michel Vautrot is a big man (6'11", 193 pounds) of formidable character. His integrity and courage are widely known, and his judgment on the field is practically flawless. As a result, he was selected to referee at the World Cup in Italy. From June 8 to July 8, 1990, 12 Italian cities hosted the 51 matches that comprise the final phase of Soccer's World Cup, played every four years. Broadcast on television around the world, these championship matches also focus attention on those who oversee the play: the referees.

Vautrot, who earns his living as a coordinator of occupational training programs for the Besançon, France, school system, volunteers his refereeing services. However, Vautrot must perform very professional duties during a match. He not only has to make sure that a game is played fairly, but with the help of two linesmen, he must also make split-second decisions without losing sight of the ball or the players on a vast playing field (measuring approximately 120 yards long by 76 yards wide). Like all athletes, he follows a tough fitness program. And as with the players he referees, a game leaves him exhausted.

A referee is constantly faced with unpredictable problems. His absentmindedness or indecision can quickly turn a match into a brawl. Against potentially over-

> *The Federation's choice of sending Vautrot to Bogotá was deliberate. . . . His integrity and courage are widely known, and his judgment on the field is practically flawless.*

whelming opposition, his only weapons are the whistle with which he halts play, the yellow card that signals an official warning to an erring player, and the red card he waves to throw a man out of the game for misconduct. Because a single victory or defeat can mean the teams' winning or losing millions of francs, a referee can't make a mistake. "When a player muffs an easy goal, he's clumsy," says Vautrot. "When a referee makes a mistake, he's dishonest."

In September 1989 in Paris, Vautrot awarded Paris-Saint-Germain, playing against Bordeaux, a penalty shot (which usually means a goal). Bordeaux goalie Joseph-Antoine Bell and his teammates instantly surrounded the referee, reviling him and trying to force him to reverse a decision that most people, including the fans, thought was unfair. Vautrot didn't flinch. He stuck to his decision and waited calmly for the storm of protest — which reached hurricane force in the Bordeaux locker room after the game — to die down. The next day a television replay of the match clearly proved he had been right. "You are always subject to intimidation on the field and off," says Vautrot. "They gang up on you, insult you, even threaten you."

> "You are always subject to intimidation on the field and off," says Vautrot. "They gang up on you, insult you, even threaten you."

After a Greek national team was eliminated in October 1985 from the European Cup match in Athens, the team's owner, a shipping magnate, stormed into Vautrot's dressing room with a pistol in his belt, yelling that he was not going to help the referee elude the furious fans outside. Vautrot managed to reach shelter in his hotel, where he spent a nervous night guarded by soldiers stationed outside his door. "I've never been afraid physically," he says, "except maybe the day in Marseille when a lead ball fired from a slingshot whizzed by a fraction of an inch from my face. If it had hit me, I'd have been dead."

Vautrot probably owes much of his skill in controlling inflamed situations to his difficult childhood. Born in Antorpe, a village in the Jura Mountains, on October 23, 1945, Vautrot was two years old when his parents separated. Five years later doctors found a murmur in his heart, compounded by rheumatic fever that confined him to his room for months. "The slightest infection caused me terrible problems," he recalls. "My first stretch in bed at my grandparents' house lasted for six months, and a second siege, eight months."

Every day while lying in bed Michel read newspapers, magazines and books. He began to idolize top athletes. At age eight, when he was finally able to go to Besançon to live with his mother, he attended the local soccer team's matches.

At 13 he was asked to write an article for the soccer magazine *Allez Besançon* on the history of the Roubaix-Tourcoing club coming to play in Besançon. "Of course, I had all the files at home," he says. At 15 he became the magazine's editor. Still banned by doctors from active sports — he was to remain under treatment until he was 25 — he joined the Franc-Comtois Racing (soccer) Club, and at 16 was named a representative on its governing board.

At club meetings he mingled with prominent professionals in the region and discovered that they often unfairly blamed referees for their team's losses. One day, overcoming his shyness, he openly defended a ref. "Shut up, kid," a veteran board member interrupted. "You don't know what you're talking about."

"What do you mean?" Michel retorted. "I'm already studying for the refereeing exam!"

In truth, Michel had never before seriously thought of becoming a ref because of his fragile health. But to make good on his word, he took the exam in 1963. His grades were so high that Octave David, a representative of the referees commission for the soccer league of Franche-Comté, resolved to make a great referee out of young Vautrot. He convinced Michel's mother to discuss the matter with the family doctor. Since the physician knew little about soccer, he thought a referee just stood quietly in the middle of the field and watched the players run around him. "Why not?" the doctor agreed. "It will get him out in the air." And he signed the necessary medical permit.

Continuing his medical treatment helped Vautrot overcome his physical handicap. Thus began the career of
the man who was to become the world's best soccer
referee. Vautrot climbed the ladder amazingly fast, six
rungs in six years to make his national first-division
debut in 1972, when he was only 27. Three years later,
at 30, he refereed his first international match, a record
in the profession.

"My trade is my living," Vautrot says. "Through soccer
I discovered life." To devote his life to his career, he has
remained a bachelor. A member of the Besançon anti-
smoking committee, he drinks neither alcohol nor coffee.
As his referee activities take him away from his office so
much, he spends his leisure time reviewing his files, while
his colleagues go on vacation. He also answers the many
letters he receives and crisscrosses France, lecturing on
the art of refereeing. "I often think of the men who referee minor-league matches," he tells his young admirers.
"They have no linesmen to help them, no police protec-
tion, no wire fence between them and the public. Those
men have real courage."

There is something uniquely commanding about
Vautrot's mere presence on a soccer field. His imposing
figure, his long stride, his imperious gestures and his whis-
tle-blowing, reputedly "the most powerful" in the country,
all combine to make his wizardry work and command
respect. When a game ends, players he has just penal-
ized rarely criticize him or complain that he was unfair.

As Vautrot sees it, the referee is the player's friend, not
his enemy. "Penalizing for the fun of it is ridiculous," he
says. This is probably why most players are pleased
when they hear that Michel is going to referee their
match. "He doesn't eye the players contemptuously; he
respects them," says France's Patrick Battiston.

Because he is so admired, Vautrot has been asked to
arbitrate matches all over the world. But he is proudest
of his five French Cup finals — played in 1979, 1982,
1983, 1984 and 1987 — which he calls his "five days of
glory." Played in June in the Parc des Princes stadium in
Paris, the French Cup is the season's high point, attended
by the President of France, members of the cabinet,

50,000 delirious fans and all association soccer writers, not to mention the millions watching on TV. In 1979, when then French President Valéry Giscard d'Estaing came to shake hands with him before the game, Michel told him, "Knowing how much trouble it is directing 22 men, I can imagine how hard it is to lead 50 million."

Michel Vautrot was chosen as the world's best referee for 1988 by a jury of sportswriters and soccer experts from some 90 countries. But the honor didn't go to his head. "I was the best in '88? Fine," he said. "But now I start over again from scratch."

The same jury conferred the honor on him again in 1989. As do compliments from players, this tribute touched him deeply. Yet Vautrot knows that the public is fickle. Just after refereeing the 1988 European Championships in Munich, Vautrot officiated at a humdrum second-division match in Montceau-les-Mines. "I was given a princely welcome," he says. "Everyone complimented me on my final. And then the home team was beaten. Naturally, it had to be my fault. After the game nobody knew me, and when I reached the parking lot, my car had been scratched up."

"I sometimes dream of being an orchestra conductor. With a good conductor, the musicians outdo themselves. It's exactly the same in soccer."

The incident saddened Vautrot, but it did not change his positive attitude toward his work. "I'm there," he says, "to protect the game and the players. I sometimes dream of being an orchestra conductor. With a good conductor, the musicians outdo themselves. It's exactly the same in soccer."

No one doubted that when Michel Vautrot refereed the 1990 World Cup match in Italy, he would do justice to his own legend.

Michel Vautrot refereed many games of the 1990 World Cup, including the opening match between Cameroon and Argentina. In this event he had to expel two of Cameroon's players for rough play in keeping with the directives of FIFA, world soccer's governing body. He described this incident as his worst memory of his international career when he announced his retirement in December, 1990. He later went on to become president of the French referees commission.

ANOTHER SIDE OF MICHAEL JORDAN

by Bob Greene

There's more to Jordan than meets the eye. The basketball superstar saves some of his greatest moves for off the court.

SOMETIMES, when you least expect it, someone comes along to change the way you look at the world. For more than 20 years, I had been writing a syndicated newspaper column, mostly reporting on the grimmer aspects of humanity. Then, in the spring of 1990, a story unexpectedly took me to a basketball game at Chicago Stadium, where I met Michael Jordan.

His balletic grace and exceptional basketball skills as a guard for the Chicago Bulls had already made Jordan, then 27, perhaps the most famous athlete in the world. We talked only briefly that day, but Jordan invited me to come see him again after other Bulls games. Over the next two years I would be present to watch Jordan achieve his greatest professional successes. But more important, I would come to know the remarkable person inside the glamorous international star.

One November night, Jordan and I found ourselves alone, and he told me about being cut as a sophomore from his high-school basketball team in Wilmington, N.C. "The day the cut list was going up, a friend — Leroy Smith — and I went to the gym to look together," Jordan recalled. "If your name was on the list, you made the team. Leroy's name was there, and mine wasn't. I went through the day numb. After school, I hurried home, closed the door to my room and cried so hard. It was all I wanted — to play on that team."

At the end of the regular season, Jordan worked up the nerve to ask the coach if he could ride along on the bus with the team to the district tournament. "I just wanted to watch the others," he explained. The coach agreed. But only if Jordan would carry the players' uniforms.

"So that's what I did," said Jordan. "I walked into the building carrying the uniforms for the players."

After a pause, he added, "It's probably good that it happened. It made me know what disappointment felt like. And I knew that I didn't want that feeling ever again."

The summer after he was cut, Jordan practiced diligently every day. The next year he made the varsity, and after graduation he went on to the University of North Carolina, where, in his freshman year, his team won the national collegiate championship.

One November night, Jordan and I found ourselves alone, and he told me about being cut as a sophomore from his high-school basketball team ...

Carmen Villafane was the first to teach me about another side of Michael Jordan. I first noticed Carmen sitting behind the Bulls' bench at a game. It was obvious she suffered from severe disabilities. Her arms and legs were subject to violent spasms, so she was strapped to a wheelchair. Her face would often twitch uncontrollably.

Gradually we started to talk. Born with cerebral palsy, Carmen had been a quadriplegic all her life. She told me that her father drove her to the games each evening.

"Is your dad a member of the Bulls' staff?" I asked.

"No," she said.

"Well, you sure have a great seat."

She broke into a big grin, and told me her story. The year before, her parents bought tickets to bring her to a game during the week of Valentine's Day. Her wheelchair had been placed on the main floor. When the teams came out before the introductions, she tried to steer herself up close to the Bulls' bench. "I want to give a valentine to Michael Jordan," she told the security guards. They allowed her to move closer.

"I gave the card to Michael," she said, her eyes tearing up even now as she recalled the moment. "He said, 'Is this for me?' I was too excited to say anything. I nodded. He opened it, read it right in front of me and then thanked me."

Not long afterward she met Jordan at an auto show where he was making a promotional appearance. He recognized her and told her he'd been looking for her at the stadium. "Where have you been?" he said. When Jordan found out Carmen had had a ticket only to that one game, he gave her his office phone number. He told her to call any time she wanted tickets.

Bulls games are usually sold out well in advance, and Carmen didn't hold out much hope that tickets would really be available. But when her parents contacted Jordan's office, a woman answered, "Oh, yes, Michael told us you might be calling," and tickets were provided.

So, Carmen went to several more games that year. Then, late the next summer, a thick set of tickets came in the mail, accompanied by a letter. "I hope you enjoy the season ahead," it said. "I'm looking forward to seeing you at every game. Michael."

Now I stood behind the bench listening to her tell me all this. As the team came out of the locker room, I looked over at Jordan in his white warm-up suit. For all the times we'd talked, he'd never said a word about this.

As that 1990–1991 season progressed, Jordan and the Bulls built up an impressive record, and fans began to believe the team could win the first championship in its

history. One March evening I got to the stadium long before game time, and Jordan was already warming up on his own. Suddenly, he motioned two teen-age ball boys to guard him. They glanced at each other. They were accustomed to shagging balls for him, but tonight he was inviting them to play. So they faced off.

Jordan drove on them. He made his first shot, then tossed the ball to one of them. The two boys dribbled and passed, while Jordan chased them into a corner and slapped the ball out of their hands. He scooped it up and spun past the boys with a between-the-legs dribble. He was laughing — as happy as I'd ever seen him on this court. But all the while, Jordan was sending an unspoken message to the boys that they were good enough to play with him. They loved it.

Earlier that season, I had written about a random act of kindness I had seen Jordan do for a child outside the arena. The day after my column ran a man called me. "I read what you wrote about Jordan," he said. "I thought I should tell you what I saw."

Here it comes, I thought. *Write something nice about someone, and people call to say the person is really a creep.* Instead the caller said that he and his wife had been to a

Michael Jordan
in a quiet moment

Bulls game, and their car had broken down in a bad area near the stadium. They were waiting for a cab to take them home when they noticed Jordan's car under a street light. "He was standing next to it, just talking with a couple of boys from the neighborhood. I thought it was nice of him," the caller said, "but I wondered why he stopped."

Later I asked Jordan whether he had been talking to those two boys that evening.

"Not two," Jordan said. "Four." Then he named all of them. He explained that the year before he'd seen the boys waiting outside the stadium in terrible weather, wanting a glimpse of the Bulls as they arrived for a game.

"I said, 'Don't wait out there. Come inside.' I brought them in with me to the game."

The boys, he said, lived four blocks away from the stadium in a dismal and dangerous area that basketball fans drove through on nights of games. "Now they wait for me on that corner every night."

And after games some nights he stops?

"Every night," he said. "They're just kids who seem like they really need someone to talk to. What does it cost me? A couple of minutes? If I went home knowing that they were still standing there waiting, it would ruin my evening."

A few nights later I ran into Jordan's wife, Juanita, at the stadium. "It's really a thing with Michael," she said. "Those four boys are on that corner every night. I think he's concerned they may be letting it take over their lives. So lately he's asked to see their school grades. If one or two of them need tutoring, he wants to make sure they get it."

As March turned to April, the playoffs began. In the 25-year history of the Chicago Bulls, the team had never advanced to the NBA finals. But Jordan and his teammates easily defeated their first three opponents, and found themselves up against the Los Angeles Lakers in a best-of-seven series for the championship.

As excited as the city of Chicago was, though, Jordan seemed almost subdued. In his first few years with the

Bulls, he had been the only star on a mediocre team. Now, at last, he had a chance for a championship. Yet when reporters asked him about the greatest prize his profession had to offer, his words were almost mechanical. I found it hard to understand.

The Bulls split the first two games of the series with the Lakers and flew to Los Angeles, where Chicago won the next two contests. With one more game remaining out West, the Bulls were a single victory from the championship. But with 6:47 left in the fourth quarter the Lakers managed to take a 91–90 lead. Their fans began singing and waving their fists.

During a timeout, I saw Jordan, furious and agitated, talking rapidly to his teammates. At that moment he was as intensely focused as any person I had ever seen. He was not going to allow his team to lose. In the final minutes the Bulls pulled away. Then the buzzer sounded: Bulls 108, Lakers 101.

... when reporters asked him about the greatest prize his profession had to offer, his words were almost mechanical. I found it hard to understand.

After the game, millions of television viewers around the country saw Jordan sitting in front of his locker-room cubicle, embracing the world-championship trophy, weeping uncontrollably as he rested his head against it. Suddenly I understood. There are only two reasons for us not to be able to talk about something: When it means nothing to us. And when it means everything.

The next year would bring another championship to Michael Jordan and the Bulls. But as I left Los Angeles in 1991, I thought about Carmen, and about the ball boys who got to play with Jordan, and about the four boys who waited under the street light for the man they trusted to come and see them.

The scoreboard in Los Angeles said that the Bulls had just become the best team in the world. But there was something more important that I had learned over the course of my time with Jordan: The real championships in life are not always won on a basketball court.

FOUR FOR THE GOLD

by William Gildea

These four athletes exemplified the Olympic spirit in the 1984 games, adding all-out determination and hard work to their talents.

FOR TWO WEEKS beginning July, 29, 1984, the Games of the XXIII Olympiad in Los Angeles held the world's attention. To compete in these Games was to respond to the charge of the modern Games' founder, French Baron Pierre de Coubertin: "The important thing is not the triumph but the struggle." Only by the most intense, all-consuming dedication would anyone reach the victory stand.

Tracy Caulkins, Swimmer

At age 12, Tracy Caulkins competed in her first senior national swim meet, finishing 52nd out of 52. Not liking to lose, she went to work with a rare determination.

Within three years, Tracy was national champion and record holder in four events: the 100- and 200-yard breast stroke, and the 200- and 400-yard medleys — butterfly, backstroke, breast stroke and freestyle.

She was up at 5 A.M. six days a week, swimming 12 miles a day — 1,700 hours in the pool a year. When she broke an ankle in September 1977, Tracy trained with a fiberglass cast, increasing her arm strength dramatically.

The freckled, blue-eyed girl with the sweet Tennessee drawl was like a shark in the water at the 1978 World Championships in West Berlin. As the then-dominant East Germans looked on in disbelief, 15-year-old Tracy won five gold medals. Early the next year she became the youngest athlete to win the James E. Sullivan Award as America's outstanding amateur athlete.

After that extraordinary crest of physical and emotional readiness, Tracy had her dreams shattered: Russian troops invaded Afghanistan, and the United States boycotted the 1980 Olympics in Moscow. Four years of hard training for nothing!

Tracy continued to win races, but her motivation suffered badly. She would have to peak all over again for the '84 Olympics in Los Angeles. That was so far away!

Still, by 1982 she had become the nation's winningest swimmer ever, surpassing Johnny Weissmuller by capturing her 37th national title. But she won only two bronze medals at the 1982 World Championships. In this painfully protracted span between Olympics, a swimmer less dedicated than Caulkins might have sunk from sight, given the competition. As swimming coach Frank Keefe puts it, "The supply of talent is so large that any given week you can have a new star. You can be on top one week and on the way down the next." Tracy endured.

By the fall of 1983 she had begun to zero in mentally on the L.A. Games. "Now I'm more of an underdog," said America's greatest female swimmer. "People aren't expecting me to do as well. But I'll do all I can."

No matter how she fared in Los Angeles, Tracy Caulkins could take immense satisfaction in simply being there. "I've never come close to swimming a perfect race," she says. "That's my goal."

> *... by 1982 she had become the nation's winningest swimmer ever, surpassing Johnny Weissmuller by capturing her 37th title.*

In the 1984 Olympics, Tracy Caulkins won three gold medals. She retired after the Olympics at age 21 to finish a journalism degree. Caulkins became the most decorated swimmer in U.S. history, breaking 63 U.S. records, five world records, and two Olympic records, and winning 12 NCAA championship and 48 national titles. She was awarded the Broderick cup and, in 1985, was voted Tennessee amateur athlete of the year. She was inducted into the Florida Sports Hall of Fame in March, 1988, the U.S. Olympic Hall of Fame in Minneapolis in July, 1990, and the International Swimming Hall of Fame in Fort Lauderdale in May, 1990.

Willie de Wit, Boxer

Boxing is full of surprises. Case in point: Willie de Wit, the 23-year-old amateur heavyweight pride of western Canada. The 6-foot-2½-inch, blue-eyed, blond-haired bomber received his first boxing lessons in a back-yard gym in tiny Beaver Lodge, northern Alberta, from a transplanted Louisiana dentist. Then, in a back room of a women's fitness center in Calgary, he learned more from Mansoor Esmail, a Ugandan expatriate taught to box by former dictator Idi Amin.

Willie quickly absorbed their knowledge. In his first fight, at a provincial tournament in Medicine Hat, he surprised himself by knocking out his opponent in 20 seconds. The coaches of every other fighter in his division promptly withdrew, giving Willie a quick title.

In June 1982, fighting for the North American amateur heavyweight title against Cuba's Pedro Cardenas in Las Vegas, Willie hammered Cardenas to the canvas in round two.

By 1984 Willie ranked as the No. 1 amateur heavyweight in the world, having the previous year defeated then No. 1, Aleksandr Yagubkin of the Soviet Union, on a decision, and knocked out No. 3-ranked Aurelio Toyo of Cuba. In addition, Willie beat the best U.S. amateur heavyweights, including Henry Tillman, and ranked as the favorite to win Olympic gold in 1984.

"Willie used to fight like Rocky Marciano, you know, a brawler," said Esmail. "Lately, he has been improving on his technique. He reminds me a bit of Joe Louis." Little wonder Willie's mother, Christina, said, "I used to worry about Willie. Now I worry about his opponents."

When Willie decided he wanted to turn down an athletic scholarship to play quarterback for the University of Alberta and become a boxer instead, Christina helped him with his exercises at home in Grand Prairie, some 320 miles north of Edmonton. While Willie would lie on his back on the dining-room table, his upper body hanging backward over the edge, Christina would hold his legs down as he did repeated sit-ups.

Grim, sub-zero winter mornings did not deter Willie from his daily training runs. Sometimes his hair would be frozen when he came back.

None of Willie's supporters expected any surprises in Los Angeles — he'd beaten all the contenders. "I think he'll win a gold medal and I think that's only Chapter One in the story," said Willie's coach Harry Snatic. Willie planned to turn pro later that year.

Willie de Wit won the silver medal in the 1984 Olympics. (The gold medal went to American Henry Tillman.) De Wit's 67–12 amateur record was the best in the history of Canadian boxing. After the 1984 Olympics, he began a three year professional boxing career during which he racked up twenty wins, one loss and one draw. De Wit then studied law, graduating from the University of Alberta in April, 1994. He was honored by the Alberta Sports Hall of Fame in May, 1995.

Kim Jin Ho, Archer

Hour after hour, arrow after arrow, Kim Jin Ho worked every day at the Taenung training center outside Seoul, South Korea. Lost in concentration, she aimed, shot, aimed and shot, walked to and from the target, suppressed the boredom, focused on winning. In archery, success depends on toughness, mind over matter.

At 6:30 each morning, Jin Ho began her day with "image training." Closing her eyes, she *imagined* every aspect of archery: bow and arrow, stance and aim, distance, target, draw, release. Seeing the bull's-eye with all the arrows drilled through it, she smiled.

After dinner, she took up "night concentration training." As the light grew fainter, she continued shooting until there was nothing left to see, only a bull's-eye to imagine. Yet her accuracy was scarcely affected; her rhythm remained the same because she had achieved, according to her coach, Kim Hyung Tak, "an emptied-mind situation." He was paying her the ultimate compliment as an archer: her mind contained no distraction to prevent a perfect shot.

> *As the light grew fainter, she continued shooting until there was nothing left to see ... Yet her accuracy was scarcely affected: her rhythm remained the same.*

The 1984 Olympics was an important event to Koreans. With Seoul the scheduled site of the 1988 Summer Olympics, South Korea wanted to make a good showing in Los Angeles. Its hopes centered on archery. At 5-foot-4, 126 pounds, 23-year-old Kim Jin Ho seemed almost too petite and shy to carry the burden of a nation. But then, wryly, she reminded those around her that "the strong *mind* wins."

In 1983 Jin Ho became the first woman ever to score more than 2,600 points — archery's equivalent of running a mile in less than 3 minutes, 50 seconds — in world-championship competition. Her score of 2,616 virtually matched those of America's two great male archers, Rick McKinney and Darrell Pace. McKinney considered Jin Ho "probably more precise, more methodical, than anyone in the world."

She was born and raised in the town of Yech'on, 100 miles southeast of Seoul. Nicknamed "the village of the bow," Yech'on has for centuries been a center for archery. Jin Ho took up the sport in the eighth grade. At age 15, she won the individual women's national championship.

With two gold medals at the 1978 Asian Games, she became a national hero. Her performance stirred new interest among young Korean women, and more began taking up the Western-style bow, which is used in international events but was new in Korea.

In April 1981 a severely pulled muscle knocked Jin Ho out of most competition for a year. "I cried a lot," she says. "It was a troubled year." But in July 1982 the muscle healed, and she set three world records in the first Asia–Oceania Target Archery Championships. In 1983 she won the world title.

Would she take the Olympic gold? Jin Ho maintained a discreet silence, living up to an archery dictum learned from her elders: Only when one is truly humble can one gain the needed powers of concentration.

Kim Jin Ho finished third in the 1984 Olympics, but set a new Olympic record in the women's 60-meter double round event. She took part in many more archery competitions, including the world championship archery

competition in 1985, at which she came in third place. In the 1986 Asian games she took two gold medals, one silver medal, and set three new records.

Daley Thompson, Decathlete

In Los Angeles in 1984, 25-year-old Daley Thompson was favored to successfully defend the decathlon title he won at the 1980 Olympics in Moscow, a title recognized as going to the greatest athlete in the world. Only one other athlete had won two Olympic decathlon gold medals: America's Bob Mathias, in 1948 and 1952.

No one who knew the muscular, 6-foot-1, 187-pound Daley considered his dream impossible. "He's the most dedicated athlete I've ever known," said American decathlete John Crist, who trained with Daley. "He lives it, loves it. And he works harder than anybody else." Daley worked out up to eight hours a day, usually seven days a week. He'd done this for ten years! He neither drank nor smoked, and regularly declined offers to endorse products. His only business was the decathlon.

Born in London in 1958, Francis Morgan Thompson

was the son of a Nigerian father and Scottish mother.
Called by a Nigerian name, Ayodele, he eventually
became Daley. A difficult child, he was expelled from
nursery school at the age of three for fighting. At seven,
he was shipped off to a boarding school whose head-
master channeled his energies into the local athletics
club. Thompson soon became a standout sprinter.

In 1974 Daley met track coach Bob Mortimer, who
saw in him a combination of height, weight, strength,
jumping ability, speed — all perfectly suited to the
demanding decathlon. Derived from the Greek meaning
"ten events," the decathlon consists of, on the first day,
100-meter dash, long jump, shot put, high jump and 400-
meter run; and, on the second day, 110-meter hurdles,
discus, pole vault, javelin and 1,500-meter run. In 1984
the record for points in the decathlon's complex scoring
system was 8,779, held by Olympic hopeful Jurgen
Hingsen of West Germany, whom Thompson had defeated in all eight of their meetings.

Daley won his first decathlon competition in Wales at
16. He made the British Olympic team the following
year, finishing 18th at the 1976 Montreal Games.

In July 1980, in rainswept Lenin Central Stadium, Daley
won the Olympic gold medal. Then he went into training
for the Los Angeles Olympics, four years ahead, dreaming
of matching Mathias's record — and of beating it in 1988.

"When you talk about the six or ten best decathletes
in the world, the only difference is in mental application,"
Daley said. "The guy who'll win is the guy who *knows*
he's going to win." Did Daley know? He wasn't saying,
but a friend revealed: "He's said it won't even be close."

---

*Daley Thompson did win the 1984 Olympic decathlon, setting a new world
record at 8,847 points. In the 1988 Olympics, Daley finished third after injur-
ing his thigh and hand in the pole vault section of the competition. Before
ending his 17-year international career in 1992, Thompson set four
Decathlon world records, won two Olympic titles, one World Championship,
two European titles and three Commonwealth Games titles. After retiring,
Thompson took up competitive driving, taking part in the National Saloon Car
Cup in May, 1993. In 1994, he began training to play professional football
and signed to play for a minor league team in 1995 at the age of 37.*

THE LADY
IS A CHAMP

by Bob Ottum

Driving through open seas at more than 90 MPH, drilling into waves that pack the power of giant pile drivers, Betty Cook has proved herself a fearless force in the macho world of ocean powerboat racing.

THE WIND WAS in full cry, stacking angry waves with white claws curling from their tops. Betty Cook's powerboat had been thrashing along for 95 miles when suddenly, after leaping from the top of one wave, the boat drilled another. Inside the wave, there was a flash impression of a perfectly quiet green world. But the impact slammed the driver's head against the hatch, then forward into the wheel.

The inside of Cook's crash-helmet face mask was coated with a red fog—she was exhaling blood from cuts inside her mouth. She tried to hold her head still, but it started nodding uncontrollably from exhaustion. Despair was closing in. It was at that moment, from high atop another crest, that the harbor came into view.

This kind of adventure is called offshore powerboat racing, and the episode described occurred off Key West

on a particularly poor November day in 1977. The nasti-
er the weather and sea, the more offshore fans love it.
And so, as the 38-foot *Kaama* came bubbling up to the
dock, they toasted the woman who was still too wobbly
to climb out of the cockpit, and nodded approvingly at
her swollen mouth.

"Where is everybody?" Betty Cook asked.

Race officials yelled that she was the first in; the others
were still out in the murk. They also noted that she was
the new open-class world champion, averaging a surprising 54.8 MPH over, under and through that wild sea.

Special Verve. Winning that 1977 race was a graduation day of sorts. It established Cook as a force in the
sport — someone to be reckoned with as an equal on a
hull-to-hull basis. Offshore powerboat racing hasn't been
the same since.

Here was an exotic sport that relished its pure-guts,
masculine image, an activity with its own language, as
foreign as Urdu, and populated by boats carrying gritty
names like *Thunderballs* and *Bounty Hunter*. And what
was this? *Kaama?* A boat named after an African antelope? As if that wasn't bad enough, apparently a lady
African antelope. The boat's foredeck featured a stylized
creature with long, graceful neck, nicely curled horns
and, well, eyelashes. And beneath that a red heart. The
racers could only nod mutely when Cook explained that
she had picked the name from a crossword puzzle and
the logo because she liked it.

Offshore racing is full of folks who are restlessly brave
and wealthy and like to prove it to one another. The
men tend to talk in capital letters and bold italics, and
most of them wear more jewelry than Cook does.

"It's an exuberant sport," Cook says. "Ocean powerboat racers operate in a dangerous element, and they
come back full of a special verve. You can't merely shake
hands with a boat racer; they're touchers. They grab and
hug. We can't stage a typical sit-down awards banquet
with these people. They're constantly up, pounding each
other and shouting. A speaker has a hard time being
heard over the din."

Through all of this, Cook was the quiet one. When she was suited up in her emotional armor, which was most of the time, there was no telling what was going on behind her ash-blond bangs and ingenuous smile. At 59, she glowed with a tan that might be called California burnish. Men found her irresistible. They swept her off her feet in giant hugs, holding her up perhaps longer than was necessary.

No False Moves. Cook won a second world championship in 1979. She captured three U.S. titles: 1978, 1979 and 1981. She also ran her own business devoted to the science of going fast over water, and she raced two boats. Both were open-class monsters powered by engines born into this world as heavy-duty Chevrolet truck blocks but emerging from Cook's engineering shop in Costa Mesa, Calif., so full of added muscle that they were fearful to behold.

The boat was capable of 100-plus MPH in the right water ... but the precise top speed was a trade secret.

One of Betty's boats was a 38-foot Scarab with a deep-V hull, and the other was a 40-foot Formula catamaran whose twin 482-cubic-inch engines spit out about 700 horsepower each. The "cat" was chock-full of what racers call Trick Stuff, graphite fibers hidden here and there, and self-contained pods to protect the crew should the boat disintegrate in heavy seas.

The boat was capable of 100-plus MPH in the right water—thrashing upwind in a moderate chop, the tunnel hull riding a cushion of air—but the precise top speed was a trade secret. Says Cook, "Once you get over eighty miles an hour on water, it's *all* fast. In fact, it's awesome."

Cook's crew consisted of fellow Californians John Connor, who handled the throttles, and navigator Dick Clark, considered a master of the art. They raced in tense, perfect harmony, giving hand signals and barking brief alerts over their helmet intercoms. All three jobs called for a delicate touch under terrible conditions.

Veteran ocean racers agree that there is a ton of difference between steering a boat and driving it; one

false move at the wheel will turn the world upside down. "Ideally, when you take off from the top of a wave, you want to land keel first," Cook says. "No corrections in midair, please. You have to dig the boat out of certain swells and guide it back up on plane. The idea is to keep the boat from hurting itself."

Ballet and Baseball. All this was happening to a slight woman whose mother wouldn't let her have a bicycle until she was 16 because it was too dangerous. As a child in Glens Falls, N.Y., Betty, then Betty Young, started ballet lessons at five, which delighted Mom, and lived a secret childhood as a shortstop on the sandlot baseball team — which delighted Dad.

The combination of activities produced a special resilience that Cook continued to have — deceptively so, because she looked so dainty. Early on racing mornings she was up and exercising. She combined lithe ballet movements with pushups and sit-ups — all done with the intensity of someone about to fight Sugar Ray Leonard. Yet when she appeared at dockside, tiny and shapely inside a bright-orange jumpsuit, there was no hint of iron. No wonder her competitors couldn't figure her out.

Tough Bernie Little, a racing commissioner and Cook's sponsor beginning in 1981, was full of admiration. "Listen," he says. "I've flown over Betty in rough water you wouldn't take a battleship out in. And I've seen her boat bounced so hard that she hit the floor, like some giant pile driver had whopped her on the head. And she pops right back up and goes on driving. I mean, you gotta hand it to that little lady."

Early on racing mornings she was up and exercising. . . . all done with the intensity of someone about to fight Sugar Ray Leonard.

Role Switch. Still, there was a time when none of this seemed remotely possible for Betty Young. After earning a bachelor's degree in political science at Boston University, she married and moved to California. There, she settled into the role of wife and mother.

Then came the day that was to change Betty Cook's life. "It was on a May morning in 1974," she says. "My husband had been racing boats as a hobby. We used our yacht as a check boat; my job was to act as hostess. But then Don Pruett, an ex-racer, convinced me that I should try racing. We used one of our race boats, a thirty-two-foot Bertram named *Mongoose*."

Pruett gave her the three most important secrets of powerboat racing: "Never turn on the top of a wave; never let go of the throttles; and always, always run in green water (that is, stay away from the wakes of other boats)."

Three days later Cook won her rookie race, a 60-mile dash from Long Beach to the Newport Beach buoy and back. She averaged 40 MPH "in a boat that was capable of eighty," she says.

Improving the Breed. By the early 1980s everything was more intense. The speeds, the rewards — and the risks — had all gone up. She was playing a high-stakes game. Figure more than a quarter-million dollars to buy and race an offshore boat for one season, and figure on blowing up a lot of equipment en route to the title. What comes out of it, as in auto racing, is a gradual improvement of the breed. Cook's Kaama Marine Engineering, Inc., was converting the lessons of racing into a new propulsion system.

Behind her animated exterior, Cook managed to mask her irritation at being constantly referred to as a racing grandma. On August 27, 1978, off the coast of England, Cook and crew raced the *Kaama* 230 miles from Cowes to Torquay and back, slamming along at a course-record 77.42-MPH average, and the London *Daily Express* headlined: IT'S GRANNY POWER AS BETTY RULES THE WAVES.

> *Behind her animated exterior, Cook managed to mask her irritation at being constantly referred to as a racing grandma.*

"One cannot help but notice the irony in this," she said wryly. "Many of the men I raced against were grandfathers, but do you ever see 'Racing Grandpa Wins Race'? Ah, well."

"Did I Do That?" Besides, at full blast, there was no hint of any grandmotherliness in Cook. She had been shaken loopy-legged in several races and once had the wind knocked out of her; John Connor eased up slightly on the throttles until she shook her head groggily and gave the thumbs up. Another time, the boat came off the crest of a wave so hard that the landing broke one of her ribs.

"I tried shouting to John to tell him," she says, "but in those heavy seas he didn't catch it. So we went slamming on. Then we blew an engine and stopped. The pain was terrible."

But that same evening, walking gingerly and fending off all huggers, she showed up at the awards banquet, sporting an off-the-shoulder gown, to congratulate the winners.

That sort of steely dedication, plus the technical advances she brought to the sport, have accorded Cook acceptance and affection in what was once a man's preserve. Jerry Jacoby, when he was the 1982 defending world champion, said, "Betty Cook has done more for this sport than just about anybody. She's a fabulous competitor. You got all these macho guys banging around the open ocean in all kinds of conditions, and here's this little lady — often beating them."

Although much of Cook's time has been spent supervising the technology that may one day change boating — and racing — she has found the sport itself a world of wonders. "Whenever we won a race, I would jump up and down in the cockpit. I'd say, 'Gee! Did I do that?'" She sure enough *did*.

GEORGE ALLEN'S LAST SEASON

by Jennifer Allen

**Critics said he was too old, too tough, too
difficult. In fact, they said, the whole idea
of his coaching a college team was ridiculous.
Would they be proven correct?**

THE LOCKER ROOM of California's Long Beach
State 49ers was so deathly quiet the dejected
players could hear water dripping in the showers after their 59–0 drubbing by the Clemson Tigers that
fall day in 1990.

The defeat was no big surprise really. It was a contin-
uation of recent history. The 49ers had not had a winning
football season in four years.

The team's new head coach, George Allen, listened
for a few minutes as his assistants yelled at the battered,
exhausted 49ers, reminding them of their mistakes — the
broken plays and missed tackles. Then he called a halt
to the criticism, knowing that the ragtag, undisciplined
bunch had little self-confidence and didn't need to feel
any worse.

"This is a lesson in life," he said. "Sometimes you're outmatched. You played a hard game, the best you could, and I'm proud of you. You should be proud too."

The pep talk was vintage George Allen. As a former coach in the National Football League (NFL), he had taken two losing teams — the Washington Redskins and the Los Angeles Rams — and turned them into Super Bowl contenders. He had compiled a personal streak of 16 consecutive winning seasons as a head coach.

Despite all his successes, however, he had been fired repeatedly by NFL owners, all of whom said they had difficulty with a man who insisted on doing things his way, and his way only. In 1990, after 21 years in the NFL and two years in the U.S. Football League, George Allen retired from coaching, seemingly forever.

But Long Beach State officials, who a few years earlier had almost canceled the school's sorry football program altogether, persuaded him to accept the toughest job of his long career. At age 72, Allen could have opted for watering his backyard fruit trees, but coaching was his true terrain. "The individual who uses the ability he was given when he was put here on earth — who works to the very limit of that ability — is doing what the Lord intended," he said. "That is what my life is all about."

To many the idea was ludicrous. If NFL team owners found Allen's style extravagant, how could he manage on a college campus? How could a seemingly over-the-hill coach who was accustomed to total obedience from veteran players deal with restless youths with ponytails and earrings? Long Beach State officials were convinced, though, that if Allen couldn't turn the school's hopelessly losing football program around, nobody could.

George Herbert Allen grew up in Detroit, where his father worked in an auto plant. Watching his dad march off to his job each morning, George learned the value of hard work and consistency. In high school, he starred in football, basketball and track.

> *Despite all his successes, however, he had been fired repeatedly by NFL owners, all of whom said they had difficulty with a man who insisted on doing things his way, and his way only.*

After a stint in the Navy, Allen entered the University of Michigan. Upon completing a master's degree in education, he began to take head-coaching jobs, beginning at tiny Morningside College in Sioux City, Iowa, and later accepting a position at Whittier College in California. At both schools, Allen developed a reputation as a winner, and soon the NFL hired him — first as an assistant coach, and a few years later as head coach of the Los Angeles Rams.

Arriving at Long Beach, Allen realized the challenge he faced: little money for football, meager support, few facilities and no hope. He began by getting his players a decent locker and weight room, and hung signs everywhere: "The Difference Between Winning and Losing Is This Much," with a forefinger and thumb held close together.

Then he confronted his raw recruits and insisted that ponytails and earrings would have to go. George Allen expected discipline, and he would get it.

"This is the biggest challenge of my life," he wrote in his journal after one of his 16-hour workdays. His wife, Etty, was always there, waiting up to greet him as she had for the 39 years of their marriage. "The love affair of the century," George called it.

The Long Beach State players soon learned that George Allen demanded no more of them than he did of himself. Give everything you've got and do just a little more than the next guy, he'd say, and set the example. He had once turned down President Gerald Ford's invitation to light the White House Christmas tree because he didn't want his team to think he was "goofing off."

One summer day with temperatures in the 90s, quarterback Todd Studer and receiver Mark Seay, out getting early practice, spied a lone figure jogging. It was Coach Allen.

"Man," said Seay to Studer, "if he can do it, we can do it too."

Just when they thought Allen was about to quit, he dropped to the ground and did his daily 101 sit-ups and 51 push-ups.

Mark Seay was one of the first to discover that the coach worked just as hard for his players. The young man was visiting his sister in Long Beach when a gang battle broke out and bullets tore through the wall where Seay's niece was playing. Diving to protect the three-year-old, Seay was shot in the back. The bullet lodged near his heart and could not be removed. The university had suggested that Seay "retire," saying that playing football was potentially hazardous.

"I'll see what I can do," Allen said when the young man told him he was going to play, even if he had to transfer to another school. The next day, Allen told college officials of Seay's determination. "Mark has the will to overcome any obstacle. He's an example for all of us," he said. And the university let Seay play.

The 49ers lost their second game of the season to Utah State by 14 points. In the locker room afterward, players were joking and laughing. To Allen it was a sign his team lacked fighting spirit. For him, winning depended on will as much as talent. "You know," he told them,

George Allen
discussing a play with some of his Long Beach team members

"I don't understand how you guys can live with your-selves when you lose. I don't see how anybody can joke or laugh."

As longer, even tougher practices followed for the 49ers, sportswriters were still questioning why Allen would attempt a comeback with this team. That was affecting the players, and he called a meeting. "Hey," he told them, "we aren't going to quit because everyone says we should. We've got to stick together here. We've got to become a family."

Then, with the team woefully behind at half time in their next game, against San Diego State, Allen got what he had looked for from the start: a leader, someone to take charge. Mark Seay spoke up.

"Everyone needs to go out there and play as if this were our last game. Tomorrow is not promised to any of us," the man who once thought he might not see tomorrow told his teammates.

Although they lost, that afternoon the 49ers learned the answer to the question the coach posed after every loss: "What could we have done to win?" This time they replied, "Play hard like Mark Seay."

Coach Allen began noticing changes in his players before they did. There were little signs. After weeks of telling them, "When I coached the Redskins, everyone had his own notebook," the players now carried note-books as they entered a team meeting, ready to copy Allen's tips for winning: stick together, be positive, be on time, say please and thank you.

As he finished writing on a large chalkboard, some of the players looked at one another. *Say please and thank you?* they wondered. *On the field? At home? At school?* None of them dared to ask.

When the 49ers played the University of the Pacific, a team with one of the top-ranked offenses in the country, Long Beach State won for the first time, 28–7! Nobody that day wrote that George Allen was over the hill.

"YOU'VE GOT TO BELIEVE" was written across Allen's milk glass on the morning of the homecoming game against Long Beach State's arch rival, Fullerton

State. The year before, the 49ers were lucky if 2,000 people showed up for a game. But by kickoff time more than 6,000 were already jammed into the stands.

With just over two minutes left, Long Beach was trailing 35–34 and Fullerton had the ball. "We need a turnover!" Allen yelled, and whether Pepper Jenkins heard him or not, he did what was called for, stripping the ball from the Fullerton quarterback, using a technique Allen had shown him.

Long Beach State recovered the fumble, and with less than two minutes on the clock the 49ers fought toward the goal line. With six seconds left in the game, the clock running and no time outs remaining, Allen sent in the kicking team. The football was snapped and booted through the goal posts. The fans went wild. Final score: Long Beach 37, Fullerton 35.

After the game one player told reporters, "Coach Allen taught us we are never out of a game no matter how little time is left and no matter what the score." It was the same message George Allen had always used to build champions.

Minutes before the game

Allen told his players:

"Now you have a chance to prove

yourself to the world. How badly

do you want it?"

By now, it was apparent to the 49ers what it took to win: preparation, dedication, discipline and teamwork. Those characteristics came easily to Allen. But not so for these young men, many from disadvantaged circumstances. Some were hearing what no one had ever told them before, that they all had potential to be winners.

Before the season's final game, against Nevada–Las Vegas, Allen reminded everyone, "We're five and five." The team had a chance to forge a winning season, their first since 1986. They were one victory away from bringing all their work to fruition. Minutes before the game Allen told his players: "Now you have a chance to prove yourself to the world. How badly do you want it?"

For George Herbert Allen, the 49ers' hard-fought 29–20 win that day was as sweet as a Super Bowl victory. The fans chanted, "We love George!" The players poured a "victory bucket" of water over the coach's head, carried him off the field and gave him the game ball.

The season was over — a winning season for Long Beach State, and a streak of 17 straight for Allen. The team meeting room now became the career placement center, where one of his signs read: "The Difference Between Winning and Losing Is Going to Class." Coach believed in helping his young players succeed in life as well as football. For the first time in 12 months, Allen took a few days off from the field, the phones, the films, the jogging.

On the morning of New Year's Eve, only 44 days after the Nevada–Las Vegas game, the coach tuned his TV to a college football game and waited for Etty to return from a workout at the local gym. But when she entered the house, she found her husband lying on the carpet. He had died suddenly of cardiac arrest.

Across the state, Allen's players, watching the same football game, listened in disbelief as they heard the sportscaster announce the news. They returned to Long Beach State for their coach's memorial service. One of Allen's three sons, Bruce, saw to it that they rode to the service in two buses — together, as he knew his father would want them to. They listened intently as Bruce read a list his father had prepared only days before: 1. Win a Championship. 2. Have Every Player I've Recruited Graduate. 3. Build a Stadium. 4. Then Take a Tougher Job.

When George Allen was chairman of the President's Council on Physical Fitness and Sports, he wrote this: "Health, happiness and success depend upon the fighting spirit of each person. The big thing is not what happens to us in life — but what we do about what happens to us." While he was certainly a great coach, George Allen was a far greater father. I know. He was my dad.

WINNING
AT ANY AGE

by William Gildea

**Anyone in any walk of life can
learn from athletes who continue
to succeed long past their prime.**

THERE IS LITTLE in sports more inspiring than
watching great competitors who should be
"over the hill" defy all odds and win. To those of
us old enough to have cheered the same athletes when
they were young, these are their sweetest victories yet.
We celebrate their latter-day triumphs because we identify with them; we notice the lines in their faces, the gray
in their hair. We wonder: how do they do it?

Their enduring successes come as no accident.
Virtually all these overachievers have prolonged their
careers through planning and hard work. Here are six
principles that have helped aging athletes keep on winning long after most of their contemporaries have
retired. They offer anyone the key to a fuller, more
satisfying life.

Believe in yourself.

As an 18-year-old out of Terre Haute, Ind., left-handed pitcher Tommy John took knocks from critics who thought he couldn't throw fast enough to become a Major Leaguer. He proved them wrong by making the big leagues in 1963. By July 1974 he had won 124 games with the Cleveland Indians, Chicago White Sox and Los Angeles Dodgers. But his impressive career seemed to be over when he ruptured a ligament in his pitching elbow.

Surgeons reconstructed the joint with an implanted tendon from his right forearm, the first surgical procedure of its kind on an athlete. His doctors told him to look for a new line of work. But John would not.

Finally, in 1976, after extensive physical therapy, he got his comeback start with the Dodgers, but he lasted only five innings. Manager Walter Alston told John that his next start would be his last chance. Against the Houston Astros, John gave up hits to the first two batters. From the mound he saw the bullpen in action: Alston wasn't going to waste time with him if he couldn't pull himself out of the trouble. Bearing down, John got two outs but then fell behind with the next batter—three balls and no strikes.

"One hanging curve ball from the end of my career," as he puts it, John fired three straight fast balls for strikes to get out of the inning. He went on to win ten games that year and pitched in a record-tying 26 Major League seasons with a remarkable 288 career victories.

"I never doubted that I would pitch again, despite what the doctors said," John says. "I just remembered that God helps those who help themselves. I decided to help myself."

Seek reinforcement.

Like most people, older athletes often need someone to turn to for support. It could be an understanding spouse, a persevering coach, a different team. One amazing season, 42-year-old pitcher Nolan Ryan was welcomed by the Texas Rangers despite his age. At his previous club, the Houston Astros, Ryan felt

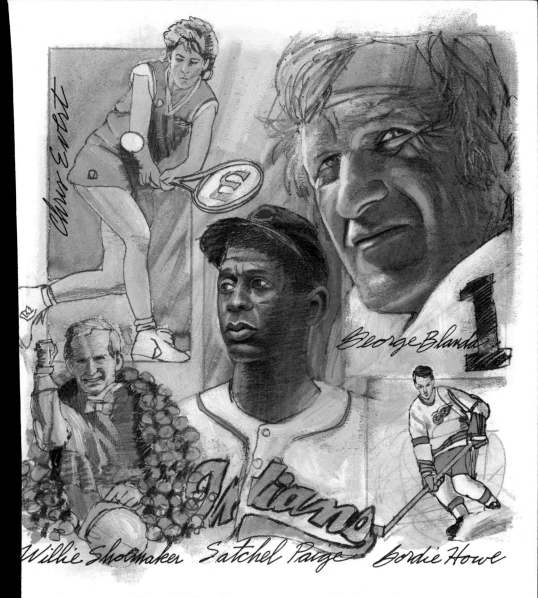

Chris Evert

George Blanda

Willie Shoemaker   Satchel Paige   Gordie Howe

"programmed" into thinking that every season might be his final one. "The attitude with the Rangers is completely the opposite," he says. "They let me know that they're behind me. It's as if they're saying, 'If he wants to pitch until he's 45, he probably can.'"

In 1989, Ryan mowed down Oakland A's Rickey Henderson with a blazing 96-MPH fast ball for an unprecedented 5,000 strikeouts in a 23-year career. He also became the oldest pitcher — by 11 years — to strike out 300 batters in a season.

Stay enthusiastic.

Ernie Banks was never satisfied playing just one baseball game a day during his glorious 19-year career with the Chicago Cubs. "Let's play two" was this Hall of Famer's eternal cry. But even the Ernie Bankses of the sporting world sometimes lose their fire. The trick is to discover a way to revive enthusiasm.

"The important thing is not to let yourself get 'down' for too long," says Banks. "It's important to keep searching for the key to success. Brooding about bad times won't help."

The best-adjusted veteran athletes keep at their sport not only for money but also for fun. Doing what makes you happy is the important thing, says legendary discus thrower Al Oerter, who won his first of four Olympic gold medals while Dwight Eisenhower was President. At 53, Oerter still beat rivals who weren't even born when he took up the sport. "People say to me, 'You're crazy,' but I'm having the time of my life!"

> *"I learned something every day," says Hall of Famer Gordie Howe, who played professional hockey for an incredible 32 seasons.*

Don't stop learning.

Realize you'll never "know it all." In his 50s, "Golden Bear" Jack Nicklaus is still an inspiration as he strides America's toughest golf courses. He is also still willing to learn.

Before the 1986 Masters, Nicklaus was doing so badly that some of his fellow pros doubted he would ever win again. Nicklaus turned to his teacher Jack Grout, who detected that Nicklaus was powering his swing with his hands instead of his whole body. The more Nicklaus practiced under Grout's scrutiny, the more fluid he felt. That bit of coaching helped make history: Nicklaus won his sixth Masters.

"I learned something every day," says Hall of Famer Gordie Howe, who played professional hockey for an incredible 32 seasons. "If I saw anything I liked watching players such as Montreal's Rocket Richard, I'd use it."

Howe never hesitated to seek guidance from coaches and teammates, and then pass it on. In 1972 he told an

11-year-old Pee Wee hockey star named Wayne, "Practice the backhand." In October of 1989, that backhand was the shot the great Wayne Gretzky used to break Howe's all-time NHL career scoring record.

Make adjustments.
When he was 39, George Blanda was cut by the Houston Oilers. Too old, they said. But the Oakland Raiders were willing to take a chance on him — if he would accept a job as substitute quarterback and kicker. Blanda figured the role of backup would at least give him the chance to show he still had plenty of football life left.

He was right. In 1970 he won or tied five straight games with his last-second kicks or passes, becoming a hero to the over-40 set. Blanda established a National Football League record for longevity — 26 seasons — becoming the NFL's oldest player ever at 48.

In tennis, Chris Evert was a dominant figure from her teens until she retired from the pro tour at 34 — ancient in a sport in which 16-year-olds win major tournaments. She and Martina Navratilova, who was still going strong at 33, will be remembered for their great matches — and for the adjustments each made to compensate for the other's strengths. Evert won 21 of their first 25 matches. Then Navratilova adopted Evert's more disciplined approach and beat Evert 13 times straight.

Chris rebounded with a strength-gaining program to match Navratilova's power. She began holding her own with Navratilova and eventually cut Martina's advantage to 43–37 in the 80 matches they played.

Stay in shape.
Bob Boone of the Kansas City Royals and Carlton Fisk of the Chicago White Sox were both 42 in the 1990 baseball season. Each played what is the most grueling position in the game: catcher.

Boone and Fisk trained religiously. Following a night game at Yankee Stadium, Boone hurried back to his hotel room where, despite the early-morning hour, he lifted weights. "It involves discipline, but it's worth it," he says. "It keeps me in the game."

Similarly, Mike Webster, as a 37-year-old center for the Kansas City Chiefs, had stretched his football career through hard work and a stringent running and weight-training regimen, even during the off-season. Webster, who played on all four Pittsburgh Steeler Super Bowl championship teams, loathes society's penchant for writing off older people. "We have such an anti-old mind-set that we tend to put people out to pasture before their time. I was old for my job, but I didn't let myself get old."

No matter the sport, all older athletes agree on the importance of maintaining one's health and staying in shape. Satchel Paige once offered this advice on clean living: "Go very light on the vices such as carrying on in society — the social ramble ain't restful."

Twenty-two years after he last won a major golf tournament, Arnold Palmer used a five-iron for a 182-yard shot at the No. 3 hole of the Tournament Players Club at Avenel in Potomac, Md. The 56-year-old Palmer lifted the ball high into the air. It hit ten feet in front of the hole, bounced, hit the pin hard and dropped into the cup. A hole in one! Incredibly, the next day at No. 3 he did it again. Golf fans marvel at Palmer's feat. But the bottom line for Palmer and other older athletes is an exhilaration they've never known before: the realization that their best days are not all behind them.

Jockey Willie Shoemaker was never more sure of that than at age 54 when he rode Ferdinand to a surprise victory in the 1986 Kentucky Derby. Over his sparkling career, he has booted home nearly 9,000 winners. But the Derby crown was especially sweet.

"It's just a great feeling," Shoemaker said with tears in his eyes, "to be able to do that at this stage in my life."

It's a feeling that millions of us can share and savor if we are willing to get in shape, keep on learning and, most of all, believe in ourselves.